*Leaning into the Wind*

# Leaning into the Wind

A MEMOIR OF MIDWEST WEATHER

Susan Allen Toth

University of Minnesota Press
Minneapolis / London

Published by the University of Minnesota Press
111 Third Avenue South, Suite 290
Minneapolis, MN 55401-2520
http://www.upress.umn.edu

Library of Congress Cataloging-in-Publication Data

Toth, Susan Allen.
    Leaning into the wind : a memoir of Midwest weather / Susan Allen Toth.
        p.    cm.
    ISBN 0-8166-4262-1 (HC : alk. paper)
    1. Middle West—Climate.    2. Middle West—Climate—Social aspects.
    I. Title.
    QC984.M53 T68 2003
    551.6977—dc21

                                                        2003004030

Printed in the United States of America on acid-free paper

The University of Minnesota is an equal-opportunity educator and employer.

12  11  10  09  08  07  06  05  04  03                10  9  8  7  6  5  4  3  2  1

*For my adventurous daughter,*
*Jennifer Lee Toth,*
*who has never liked Midwest weather*

*When we pulled out into the winter night and the real snow, our snow, began to stretch out beside us and twinkle against the windows, and the dim lights of small Wisconsin stations moved by, a sharp wild brace came suddenly into the air. We drew in deep breaths of it as we walked back from dinner through the cold vestibules, unutterably aware of our identity with this country for one strange hour, before we melted indistinguishably into it again. That's my Middle West.*

—F. Scott Fitzgerald, *The Great Gatsby*

*The dust and heat, the burning wind, reminded us of many things. We were talking about what it is like to spend one's childhood in little towns like these, buried in wheat and corn, under stimulating extremes of climate: burning summers when the world lies green and billowy under a brilliant sky, when one is fairly stifled in vegetation, in the colour and smell of strong weeds and heavy harvests; blustery winters with little snow, when the whole country is stripped bare and grey as sheet-iron. . . . It was a kind of free-masonry, we said.*

—Willa Cather, *My Ántonia*

*The cyclone had set the house down, very gently—for a cyclone—in the midst of a country of marvelous beauty.*

—L. Frank Baum, *The Wizard of Oz*

# Contents

A Note to Other Midwesterners    *xi*

Leaning into the Wind    *1*

The Weather Was Full of Promise    *12*

Other Weather, Other Places    *24*

Storms    *39*

Down in the Basement    *55*

A Window on the Weather    *61*

Weather Words    *75*

Things That Go Buzz in the Night    *85*

A Cold-Blooded Woman    *93*

Garden Weather    *97*

The Weather Doesn't Grow Old    *111*

Who Speaks in the Pillar of Cloud?    *116*

# A Note to Other Midwesterners

I HAVE SPENT MOST OF MY LIFE in Iowa, Minnesota, and Wisconsin. Although I have traveled in many other parts of the Midwest, I cannot pretend to know them as intimately. I have drawn most of my examples from what I know, not intending to slight those states whose residents might feel ignored—except for the fact that they, too, live in the midst of Midwest weather.

# Leaning into the Wind

Weather dominates everything.
—Stephen E. Ambrose, *Nothing Like It in the World*

Racing black clouds, brilliant patches of blue sky, frosty mornings, soft dissolving nights: as I look back, I often see moments in my life in an aureole of weather. I think of a long-ago love affair that disintegrated on a hot humid afternoon, my failing first marriage punctuated by thunderstorms, my struggles as a single parent crystallized in a snowdrift towering over my freezing daughter, a terrible parting miraculously eased by the promise of that same blanketing snow.

Weather saturates my memories. Was the sun shining that afternoon? Were the stars blinking that night? Was I uncomfortably hot, or shivering in the cold, or too numb to notice? Sometimes I remember those outer temperatures almost as sharply as my inner ones. Even now, weather shakes and changes my perceptions: how I feel about the world, how I feel about myself, even what I will do next.

Consider, for instance, this gray, snow-glazed April morning. At breakfast I was grumpy and tired, having awakened several times in the rainy night before I finally got up to close the windows. Before dawn, rain turned to sleet, sleet to snow. If today were bright and clear, I would slip outdoors for a long walk, and then, revived by sun and fresh air, I might settle down to a productive afternoon. But now, staring at the dark skies and damp frosting of snow, I feel I can't possibly make much of an effort. On such a drowsily melancholy afternoon, who could work? Who could write? I think I'll take a nap.

Today's dull gloom is only a mildly disconcerting interruption, but Midwest weather can also be an intense trial, a honing of endurance skills no one asks for. Many years ago, waiting to see a man I loved for what I knew would be the last time, I spent a hot summer morning on my muddy knees in a raspberry patch. Our conversation later that day no longer haunts me, and even his face is now blurred. But if I try to recall that morning, I can immediately evoke the sun-drenched sticky air, so thick it hung about me like a gauzy damp towel. Under that relentless sun, I gathered raspberries as a test of my survival.

I do not always quail underneath the weight of Midwest skies. Our weather can be a solace as well as a trial. Some nights, when I have trouble sleeping, I search for images of overwhelming peace. Often they are intimately connected with weather. I like to picture a snowy January afternoon at our Wisconsin cottage in the woods. It is just after lunch; the clock is ticking almost inaudibly. Curled up on a sofa below a wide window, I watch the snow gently falling while a light icy wind beats against the glass. As I pull a lap robe around my ears and snuggle deeper into the cushions, I listen to the crackle of fire in our wood-burning stove.

Sometimes, shifting my collection of mental slides, I change the scene to a blazing hot summer afternoon. I see myself floating on my back in a small outdoor pool a short walk from our cottage. Outside the shimmering pool, the heat is transfixing. Everyone I pass on the road seems to move very slowly. The birds are silent, grasshoppers are in hiding, the morning bees have stopped buzzing. Even in the pool, I paddle just enough to stay afloat. The sky is shockingly blue, the water refreshingly cold. I close my eyes against the sun and drift toward the middle of a tranquil sea.

Weather, always weather: I cannot imagine a vivid moment or a passionate experience without it. And no wonder. Weather in the Midwest is high drama, moving unexpectedly from one scene to another, the sets constantly changing. Short fervent springs. Seesawing falls, dipping between summer and winter. Long cold winters. Hot humid summers. Wildly unpredictable variations of temperature, sun, wind, rain, snow, sleet, hail, and even drought. If it can happen, it will.

I know the Midwest is not the only part of the country with daunting weather. Snow buries Buffalo; heat simmers and stews in Southern bayous; sun broils Arizona; hurricanes batter the Carolinas; unseasonable frosts wither crops in Florida; sea fog isolates villages along the northern Pacific coast; earthquakes constantly threaten California; part of the Northwest sits uneasily beneath Mount St. Helens volcano; and in New England, winters can be long, springs wet, summers hot.

But Midwest weather is subtly different. Not only is it extreme, it has more scope. Weather drives in with such force, from so far away. Those of us who live here know, as surely as our feet are planted on the land, that we lie smack in the middle of the country, our flat cities, prairies, fields, lakes, all open to the elements. Nothing protects us; nothing shields us from the heat, wind, and snow that sweep across so much distance. When we see our weather coming, we know that it has traveled, gathering speed, for hundreds, even thousands of miles. It will soon slam into us like a clenched fist.

Our weather never seems merely local. It has a length, a breadth, a reach that can be both magnificent and dismaying. Nobody is quite sure where our weather starts and stops. Nothing, in fact, seems to give us any boundaries, any sense of closure, except a distant dream of mountains where the West begins. Stand outside any of our towns, where the land flows freely to the horizon, and try to imagine an end to the Midwest. Where, exactly? The Mississippi? Hudson Bay? The Gulf?

Since no one is definitive about exactly what it means, the term *Midwest* is as baggy as a large loose rubber band. It might encompass, depending on who is plucking it, such widely separated states as Ohio and North Dakota. Most people would loop in North Dakota, South

Dakota, Minnesota, Wisconsin, Iowa, Kansas, Nebraska, Illinois, Indiana, Michigan, and Missouri. A few might stretch the band to include Ohio, Oklahoma, Arkansas, even parts of Kentucky or the fringes of Montana. A literary friend in New York recently asked me if I planned to mention the weather in Colorado; she had once been there and was sure it too was "Midwest." And who knows? Maybe it is.

Most people decide what and where the Midwest is according to where they live. Many disagree. People in North Dakota may think of Ohio as "back East"; Minnesotans might refer to Missouri as "down South," and as for Colorado—well, you could try asking a man in a Stetson and cowboy boots on a Denver street if he's a Midwesterner. But we'd all probably admit that if you think you're in the Midwest, you probably are. We have a certain indefinable pride about all the territory we cover. I suspect we don't mind being called "flyover land," because, even if we're not sure who belongs in the Midwest, we know it is so big, sprawling so comfortably across so much of what we prefer to call the "heartland," that it does, in fact, take hours to fly across it. Most people know it doesn't take long to fly across Rhode Island.

Not only does our weather have an awesome scope, it has another, more dubious distinction. Compared to weather in other parts of America, it is unusually sly and tricky. Take March, for example. In my part of the Upper Midwest, the Twin Cities, early March is usually cold, snowy, and depressingly cloudy. But a few years ago in March, the sun shone with unexpected bright fury. Temperatures soared, and Minnesota seemed to cartwheel into Florida. One especially hot Sunday afternoon, when Minnesotans ordinarily might have huddled before their televisions to watch basketball, throngs poured out of their houses. On a leisurely three-mile walk around our nearby lake, I almost had to elbow my way through crowds.

As I studied the people who passed, no one looked quite normal. Even when they were smiling and talking, they seemed white-faced and dazed, as if suddenly released from silent months in underground cells. Although only a few days earlier, frozen sheets of thinning ice had covered most of the lake, now a man and a woman lay facedown, in faded swimsuits, on a warm sandy patch by the shore. Their pale skin looked as if all the color had been bleached from it by the long indoor winter. The couple looked so odd, so shockingly out of season, that many walkers slowed, or even stopped for a moment, to stare at them with amused admiration.

This unseasonable heat—sixties and seventies, almost torrid compared to our recent zero or ten below—lasted for a blissful ten days. Then, swiftly and stealthily, a new front blew in, changing everything within hours. One night, the breeze was so reassuringly mild that I left two windows open in the bedroom. Sometime during the night I felt cold and pulled up my blanket. I remember hearing a soothing patter of rain. Next morning, when I stumbled sleepily across the room, I was shocked to see that the leering red arrow of our outdoor thermometer had swung to twenty-four degrees. A light coating of new snow had brushed the front yard white again. I took a deep breath, steadying myself, as I prepared to plunge back into winter.

The next year, March was constantly and bitterly cold. Even by the end of the month, ice-hardened snow disfigured sidewalks and lawns like a grayish white fungus. Snow fell, sleet, freezing rain. Complaining about the weather, as we frequently can, Minnesotans invoked that balmy interlude. It now represented a long-gone golden age that might never come again. Buttoning our down coats against a frigid wind, we cried: "Remember last March? We had a picnic! The beer garden at the Black Forest was open! I was wearing sandals!"

Although in a few years, distracted by new anomalies, we'll soon forget one unusually warm March, we don't forget all our weather. Much of it passes into folklore. Anyone who lives in the Midwest long enough eventually absorbs at least a few of its weather legends and myths. An essential part of our communal spirit, some of these stories are documented history; others are fictional. But, like all good stories, the made-up ones linger. Whenever a tornado appears on a local radar screen, a warning siren sounds, or the television announcer fervently exhorts us to seek shelter, I often think of the inspired opening of *The Wizard of Oz*.

Who on the plains hasn't dreamed of being whirled up into a tornado? For anyone who was a child in the Midwest, Dorothy's way of traveling to Oz is almost as riveting as what happens after she arrives. When a cyclone seizes her aunt and uncle's Kansas farmhouse, the shrieking wind carries her on a swaying journey for hours. As he describes this strange magic carpet, L. Frank Baum manages to convey both its terrifying power and, at the same time, Dorothy's eventual acceptance and even enjoyment of it. "It was very dark, and the wind howled horribly around her, but Dorothy found she was riding quite easily," Baum says reassuringly, adding that Dorothy felt as if she were being rocked gently, like a baby in a cradle. Finally, with a Midwesterner's hard-earned insouciance about weather, Dorothy falls asleep.

Not long ago I saw in our local newspaper a photo of a man, hair blown by the wind, standing up in his car with his head poking through the sunroof. The sky above him was dark and threatening. He was looking intently upward, and he held a pair of binoculars ready in his hand. "George Simon," the caption read, "was studying the ominous sky near Rochester Tuesday afternoon. Simon's hobby is weather, and he likes to chase storms. A tornado alert had been issued for Rochester until midnight, and Simon was hoping to be the first to sight a funnel cloud." Here in the Midwest, I thought, weather actually qualifies as a hobby, even as enticingly dangerous fun, like an almost-out-of-control roller-coaster. George Simon and L. Frank Baum were kindred spirits.

Although in different parts of the Midwest, each generation accumulates its own tales of local legendary weather—in Minnesota, the extreme heat and cold of '36, the blizzard of March '66 (with July hailstones that year that measured as much as sixteen inches around), the late May snow in '65, the floods of '69, the long drought of '88—most of these memories soon disappear from common knowledge. But a few are so hair-raising, so emblematic of our untamable climate, that they are invoked, years later, as warnings to unbelievers. In Minnesota, as November 11 approaches, someone, somewhere—on radio or television, at a dinner table, in a school—ceremoniously retells the story of the Armistice Day blizzard of 1940.

On that November day, the weather seemed fine. Hunters, hurrying to fields and woods for the holiday, were enjoying temperatures in the sixties. Although forecasts called for a cooling trend, no one expected anything resembling winter for days, maybe weeks. But a storm moved in from the Rockies with disastrous speed; temperatures dropped precipitously; heavy snow—as much as twenty-six inches—began to fall. The blizzard that so quickly developed that afternoon killed forty-nine people in Minnesota alone. Stranded hunters, the story tells us, were found days later, frozen to death, still in their shirtsleeves.

That image—men on holiday, who in the morning may have paused, warm and thirsty, for a welcome beer, trapped that afternoon in a ferocious storm—is imprinted on our collective imagination. So each November, weather commentators and editorial writers, born long after 1940, remind us, brandishing the Armistice Day blizzard, not to take our weather for granted. Be prepared, they intone. They repeat, with grim relish, one of our Midwestern incantations: hope for the best, but expect the worst.

I have lived through many snowstorms—safe, indoors, never really frightened—but when I think "blizzard," I don't picture the cloudlike drifts outside my own door. Instead I remember vivid scenes from Laura Ingalls Wilder's classic children's book *The Long Winter.* In this fictionalized autobiography, a particularly ferocious South Dakota winter becomes a marathon of cold and snow. One monstrous blizzard follows another. When Pa Ingalls goes outdoors to feed the stock, the snow is so high and the blizzard so blinding that he has to follow his wife's clothesline to find his way back to safety.

This haunting emblem, the life-saving rope dangling somewhere in the storm—somewhere, oh pray God, but where?—recurs obsessively in Midwestern literature. In his recent memoir, *What I Think I Did,* Larry Woiwode describes brutal weather a few years ago in North Dakota: "A chill grips my back as I realize I'm at the epicenter of something worse. I can't see the closest building, not even the furnace, and think of the tales of the farmers who had their wives pay out a rope tied to their waists as they left for chores, so they were certain to find their way back, and some didn't. So their wives went to look and were lost, too." Throughout his memoir, Woiwode explores the idea of safety, where it lies and how to find it, as well as the reality of inescapable and irreparable loss. The weather in North Dakota is only part of his story.

Fortunately, not every enduring image of Midwest weather is terrifying. For moviegoers who know little about America between Pennsylvania and Wyoming, but who saw Jack Lemmon and Walter Matthau in *Grumpy Old Men,* that image might be, quite cheerfully, an ice-fishing shack. In Wabasha, Minnesota, where the movie is set, such ramshackle shelters dot the Mississippi River in winter, as they do frozen lakes and rivers in many parts of the Midwest. Lemmon and Matthau made those idiosyncratic tiny houses, devoted to almost as much drinking as fishing, into icons of male bonding, places where grown-up Tom Sawyers can hide out from women and the comfortably civilized world. Ice-fishing houses pop up on city lakes in Minneapolis soon after the first piercingly cold blasts, and when they disappear, virtually overnight, we know spring has come.

A more glamorous symbol of winter weather is the Ice Palace. In St. Paul, the city fathers long ago invented the January Winter Carnival, with parades, floats, games, and an architectural extravaganza constructed with blocks of ice. This improbable palace caught the imagination of F. Scott Fitzgerald, who enshrined it at the center of his short story "The Ice Palace." In this story, Sally Carrol, a Southern belle who becomes engaged to a young man from St. Paul, travels to St. Paul for a winter visit. As part of her introduction to the city's excitements, she is taken to the huge crystalline castle. When she finds herself accidentally lost in its labyrinthine depths, she understandably panics.

Surrounded by dark and ice, shivering with cold, Sally has an extraordinary vision. Fitzgerald knew his Midwest, and here he conveys something of the Midwesterner's sense of distance, of disconcerting weather materializing from faraway, utterly unknowable places: "She was alone with this presence that came out of the North, the dreary loneliness that rose from ice-bound whalers in the Arctic seas, from smokeless, trackless wastes. . . . It was an icy breath of death; it was rolling down low across the land to clutch at her." Although

Sally is soon rescued, she now realizes that she could never marry her fiancé. And home she goes, back to the lazy, languid South—clearly, in Fitzgerald's view, a seductive but enervating climate.

Over many years—more than fifty, and counting—of living in the Midwest, I have acquired my own highly personal bits of weather lore. They are full of contradictions. On chilly gray days, as I have admitted, I think the weather dictates a pause from normal activity. Those are the days I am almost required to sink onto the sofa for a little doze. On some of winter's coldest mornings, however, I feel a perverse need to don my multiple layers of thermal padding and go for a plodding walk. After all, I sternly ask myself, winding my muffler around my face, how can I allow the weather to defeat me?

Blessed and cursed with a highly emotional temperament, I sometimes find the weather exacerbating, sometimes calming. To my surprise, I once discovered that I particularly look forward to the first heavy white snow of early winter, because it promises a temporary peace. Anyone who has lived through a bitter Midwestern winter, its treacherously icy streets and wind like piercing needles, may wonder at the idea of its onset as soothing. But for me, it can be. I remember how, many years ago, I realized that a deep heartsickness, a pain I thought I would never recover from, could become more bearable with that first snow. Ever since then, I have thought of winter differently.

One afternoon in early fall, I sat in a therapist's office. After three years of keeping company, the man I wanted to marry and I were no longer seeing each other. Someone from his past had unexpectedly reappeared, and, as he told me, "I have to find out why I've never gotten over her." I knew that something had kept him from making a permanent commitment, but I hadn't expected this. For almost three months, we stayed apart. I felt I had waited all my life not just for someone like James, but for precisely, and only, James himself. I was forty-four, he was almost sixty. Now, after eleven years of being single, I did not have a sense of limitless time, and I could not imagine a future without him. The therapist was trying, gently, to force me to stop looking backward. She wanted me to stop grieving so keenly. What, she finally asked, could I think of that would make me feel better?

My mind swept forward. Every day, every night looked empty. I no longer relished my former single life—those undisturbed evenings to myself, solitary self-indulgent trips to London, short pickup meals during which I read the newspaper and sometimes ate with my fingers. I would discover these pleasures again, my therapist assured me, but meanwhile, what would help? Suddenly I had an answer. "The first snow," I said. "I'll feel better when the first snow comes." She too had lived in the Midwest many years. She nodded. "Yes," she said knowingly, "I think you will."

When I left her that afternoon, I puzzled over my answer. Picturing that first snow felt comforting. But why? I had never especially liked Minnesota winters. I didn't much like ice-skating, and I rarely took out my cross-country skis. My car sometimes didn't start, I had trouble shoveling my long sidewalks, I worried about fuel bills and pneumonia and dangerous driving and heavy snow on my sagging roof. Yet something deep inside me seemed to relax when I thought of seeing, just outside my window, those first thick white flakes begin to fall.

Those flakes would fall like a white curtain, closing off the rest of the world. They would cover everything. I could sense them muffling my grief, hushing my tumult, damping my sense of loss. With that first snow, I thought, summer and fall would be over. More than that might be over, or almost over. The world will be fresh and white, and I will start again.

As it happened, I did not pay much attention to the first snow that winter. A few weeks after that visit to the therapist, James called. He had made a terrible mistake, he said, and he did not want to lose me. Now that he knew, we should be married as soon as possible. Understandably wary, I wanted to wait a little, but I was willing to be persuaded. A few months later, on a cold February morning, we were married in a friend's house.

Midwest weather gave us its own peculiar blessing. As we exchanged vows, we could see out the living-room windows that a heavy, driving snow had begun to slant across the sky. We had planned a week's honeymoon in Arizona. After the ceremony, another friend drove us to the airport. Snow was piling up on the freeway, and under most circumstances, I would have been terrified. Our windshield was white and blurry, and a few cars were already in the ditch. But, as our friend steered through the whiteout with care and determination, I sat calmly in the backseat with James. I was tired, excited, happy, and, yes, a little nervous about the roads. But I felt somehow confident that we would surely make it through this snowstorm—and, with this blessing and a bit of luck, through all the unexpected weather to come.

# The Weather Was Full of Promise

That afternoon after school they all went up on the Big Hill hunting
for violets. It was one of those April days on which it seemed that
summer had already come, although the ground was still muddy and
brown.... Birds in the bare trees were singing with all their might,
and Betsy, Tacy, and Tib sang too as they climbed the Big Hill.

—Maud Hart Lovelace, *Betsy and Tacy Go over the Big Hill*

WHEN I WAS YOUNG, the weather was full of promise. Early fall
winds in Ames, Iowa, whispered of cascading leaves to be kicked into
red-gold storms, the faint flickering glow of leering orange pumpkins
on black Halloween nights, and the sudden sparkle of silvery white
frost on wet green grass. When winter puffed and blew soft snowflakes
against my window, I knew my sister and I could soon shape it into
downy cushions, scooped-out caves, and tottery snowmen. In spring,
just in time for May baskets, rain melting the last smudges of snow
would quickly unveil quivering delicate snowdrops, Dutchman's-
breeches, and woodland violets. Then I could put away my snowsuit
and run outside, quick, easy, free as a robin.

As I grew a little older, the winds of weather whirled other pleasures into my life. On Friday nights in the fall, floodlights turned
our high school football field into a gladiators' stage, filled with
frantic shouts and cheers. Sheltering from the cold darkness beyond the lights, I shivered and huddled with other girls, aflame with

excitement, singing, clapping, and rocking to the confident blare of our marching band. The frosty air only made us giddier.

On many winter days, I hurried with my mother's old ice skates down to frozen Lake La Verne, a man-made pond, where I sometimes found a few friends to play crack-the-whip. Despite my frequent stumbles, I thrilled to our speed, edged with a sense of danger. Besides, crack-the-whip was a tantalizing chance to hold hands with a boy—even if my sweaty hands were muffled in mittens. In later springs, packed into someone's borrowed car, my high school girlfriends and I would roll down its windows, drive up and down Main Street, and yell joking taunts at boys we knew in other cars. As the warm breeze whipped my carefully combed hair into unmanageable tangles, I reveled in the playful tease of summer.

Every turn of weather brought its own magic, but the few weeks of early summer were the most seductive. In the first days of June, when school was not yet out, the sun would begin to shine into our classrooms with a kind of unruly glee. With the windows open as high as the strongest boy could push, heat still poured through the room. Everyone moved uneasily on the wooden seats. Summer tickled damp strands of hair on our moist foreheads, tugged at itchy shirt collars, and lightly glued skirts to sticky thighs. Nobody paid much attention to the flapping pages of the open books on our desks or the final assignments exhausted teachers determinedly wrote on grimy blackboards. Outside, summer was calling: dew-moistened mornings, lazy basking afternoons at the city swimming pool, starry nights at the A&W root beer stand or the Ranch Drive-In Theatre.

On the day school finally closed, I was giddy with anticipation. Although, by the time I was a teenager, I knew I would be working somewhere for at least part of the summer—detasseling corn, baby-sitting, helping out at the local newspaper—I was sure I was embarking on a new adventure. Everything outside the schoolrooms was different: bright hot sun, impossibly blue skies, long days lingering into late twilight, dappled shadows of trees, emerald lawns not yet faded by a parched August. The world around me radiated a shimmering brilliance. How could weather like this not hold the promise of something wonderful?

Growing up in the Midwest, I soon came to expect the recurring possibility of transformation. Arriving with the booming timpani of a thunderstorm, the warning crackle of an unexpected frost, or a scene-shifting blanket of snow, each season offered a fresh beginning. I sensed this most deeply in the fall. On the first cold night of August, the bracing splash of air—blown, it felt, from an unfamiliar land— jolted me into the future. Although I mourned the end of summer's freedom, I started to look ahead to September. I thought of the new courses I'd be taking, the French I'd learn, the secrets of chemistry I'd master, an introductory journalism class that might be my entry to a romantic future career. I also savored the pleasurable strangeness of being a whole year older: an eighth-grader, a sophomore, and, eventually and amazingly, a senior.

The first day of school flashed like a neon number on the calendar. With late-summer temperatures soaring into the nineties, I began excitedly considering my new self. What would happen? How would my life change this year? How would I be different? I had no way of articulating my vague, half-recognized feelings. I just knew that somehow, in some way, I expected some kind of new beginning. Of course I didn't acknowledge that clearly; after all, nobody I knew in Ames in the 1950s ever talked about personal renewal. Our Presbyterian minister, Dr. Remington, certainly never ventured onto such uneasy ground. When he preached on spiritual rebirth, it sounded more alarming than exciting. Despite his exhortations about a new life in Christ, I noticed that everyone in our congregation appeared to stay more or less the same. My friend Helen, a Baptist who said she had undergone a total baptismal dunking that instantly turned you into a new person, confessed she didn't think it had worked on her.

But Midwest weather, in a peculiar way, did transform some of us. As it changed our outward appearance, it changed something more. Prompted by the climate, in the course of a single year we would shed one chrysalis after another: storm coats, rain slickers, pedal pushers, sleeveless blouses, back to sweaters. Modest as most of our wardrobes were, we had to dress several times a year in a different way. So for many of us girls, each new season required careful planning.

The first day of school, for instance, was critical. Somehow I was convinced that what I looked like that first day might determine who I'd be the rest of the school year. All summer I had hung around casually in shorts, halter tops, swimsuits. Now, with fall lurking in the air, I needed to make a different impression. Organized. Put together. Whatever I wore had to be brand-new, never before seen, fresh from our sewing machine, or, if I'd earned enough that summer, from Younkers Department Store. As I painstakingly prepared my opening costume, I wanted to look like all the other girls in their twirly skirts or neat shirtsleeve dresses. But I was acting an important new role for myself.

As the weather changed throughout the year, not only did my clothes look different, but I felt different too. In winter, bundled up in a bulky coat, scarf, and, ignominiously, warm wool slacks under my skirts—slacks quickly whipped off and slapped into my locker after I got to school—I was weighed down. I tramped, I plodded, I moved slowly. When a blizzard struck, I might be forced into a dead stop and marooned at home. Nothing was effortless.

But in early spring, trying on my new Easter Outfit, I could feel my spirits lift again. An Easter Outfit had capital letters; it signaled a turning point. Even if a razor-keen wind cut through the air, or snow flickered in the sky, an Easter Outfit, dressy enough to wear to church on Easter Sunday, had to look as if I were dancing into spring. Pastel or white or flowery. Linen, piqué, featherweight cotton. Flimsy jacket, pale shoes, shiny patent leather purse.

When everyone in church that Easter morning rose to sing my favorite hymn, "Jesus Christ is risen today, ahhhh-ah-ah-ah-ah-LAY-ee-loo-oo-ya," I dipped and soared with joyous abandon through its arpeggios. Because I had a limited semialto that couldn't edge much higher than middle G, I didn't usually like to sing in church. But on Easter, I didn't care how squeaky I sounded. I wanted to join in the celebration. Although Dr. Remington would have disapproved of how I muddled material with spiritual matters, I agreed with him that today might indeed be a rebirth.

I still cherish the elusive possibilities of new beginnings. Midwest weather is surprisingly full of hope. Each season, as the weather turns, I feel a little different, and sometimes, if I'm lucky, I can also envision my life turning, revolving, and changing direction. Much as when I was younger, I sometimes see these changes reflected in what I choose to wear. I don't like admitting this link to myself, because it feels depressingly superficial and incongruous. I am certainly not an avatar of fashion. I have never remotely had a model's figure; I haven't adjusted my hemlines for years; I think I stopped following trends somewhere back in the 1970s. No one but me (and my sweetly observant husband) has the slightest interest in what I wear.

But I like the quiet drama of costume changes, and Midwest weather gives me plenty of opportunities. With each costume, I become a slightly altered character. In winter, for example, I go into disguise. When I am walking around a Minneapolis lake in January, I am swathed and muffled. Before I leave the house, I don layer after layer of protection, building a carapace, disappearing behind it. First the lightweight long johns; then the heavy long johns. On top of those, the windproof pants. Undershirt, turtleneck. Down jacket, hood pulled up. Mittens. Scarf wrapped around my face. When I am finished, I am a life-size stuffed doll, a bumpy giant pillow, a sleeping bag with boots.

As I pass other walkers, all anyone can see of me is a slit where my eyes must be. (If the sun is out, I am wearing big dark glasses, so my eyes are undercover too.) I am so positively unidentifiable that not long ago, on just such a cold January day, one of my stepdaughters, who is quite dear to me, passed without a word. She didn't know who I was, and I wouldn't have known her, either, except I happened to recognize her little brown-and-white sheltie, who trots with a peculiar lilting gait. When I called out to Sandy and her dog, they both stopped in surprise.

When I am operating in this disguise, I am blissfully anonymous. No one will stop me; I don't have to talk to anyone. I am not a responsible person anymore. Soothed, reflective, I retreat into an inner space and let my mind drift to odd places. Since I have to keep glancing at my feet—icy patches can be treacherous—I don't try to concentrate on plans or work out solutions to anything. I just keep going, plodding happily along, occasionally wiggling my toes to make sure they are not getting too cold.

Once, at the end of a winter afternoon when the light was fading into a soft feathery pink, I stepped off the path and scrambled down to the lake itself. A wild wind had recently blown most of the snow from its surface. Since the ice was rough and corrugated, I didn't think I would need to worry too much about falling. So I struck out boldly across the frozen lake, heading in a direct line for the low shoreline on the far side that would lead me back up to a sidewalk and then home. When I was out in the middle of the lake, I stopped.

Then I realized how alone I was. Alone, and surrounded by silence. I could not remember when the world had seemed so silent. The distant cars whose yellow blinking eyes circled the lake in the dusk were as quiet as padding cats. The only sound I heard was a faint whir of wind, busily whisking up bits of loose snow that clung to the ice. If I stood here too long, I thought, I might freeze, and no one would notice for hours. After all, I was only a small dot in the middle of a vast expanse of ice. The safety of shore was probably half a mile back, half a mile forward. For just a few moments, until I began walking again—more quickly—toward home, I had become an intrepid Arctic explorer.

When the weather finally warms into spring, I turn into someone else. Off come my cozy leggings, clinging turtlenecks, and fuzzy sweaters. Now I don long loose dresses, the kind that rustle gently as I walk, and as soon as the temperature creeps up to sixty, I slip into crepe-soled sandals. I feel buoyant, gay, frivolous, yet sturdy too, as if I might now set out on a long, long walk, one that could last all morning, deep into afternoon. As I stride down the street—usually I can find, in fact, only a snatched spare hour to circle our lake—I sometimes think of Virginia Woolf. She loved to walk too, and when she stayed in her country house in Sussex, she often covered miles each day over the downs. In photographs from the 1920s and 1930s, she looks ethereal and wraithlike, awkwardly graceful, fine-boned but surprisingly strong. I picture her drifting among the flowers in the garden at Monk's House, floating across the pastures and meadows, yet determined and purposeful. I look nothing like her; I am in awe of her genius; I lack her quicksilver wit and glancing brilliance; but sometimes, just for a moment, on those first intoxicating spring days when my long skirts swoosh around my legs, I feel a little like Virginia Woolf.

In early September, I float and drift no longer. As soon as I have taken out my heavy cotton pants and hefty turtlenecks, I have become someone else: efficient, motivated, occupied. Now I don't have time to dream; I need to prepare for winter. Since I no longer take classes or teach, I do not look ahead through the narrowing focus of an academic syllabus. Instead I map out a culinary survival course. In early fall, Minnesota's tomatoes, zucchini, sweet corn, and other succulent vegetables are piled high in the city farmer's market. So I look up recipes and tie on a long splashproof apron. Then I mince, chop, sauté, stew, and make gallons of soups—corn-tomato bisque, minestrone, turnip-potato vichyssoise, creamy cauliflower. Soon I can open the door of my freezer and admire a tall stack of neat white containers, awaiting dark cold winter days. When I sashay around my kitchen, apron crackling, window open to the fresh cooling air, I am lustily cheerful as I whisk, slosh, and pour. Perhaps, just for this morning, I am Julia Child.

I wonder, if I lived in a more settled climate, whether I'd be tempted into those new identities. Once, many years ago, I lived in London for seven months, from late December to mid-July. It was a difficult time. I was teaching by day and leading student theater groups by night, coping with a restless small daughter, fighting fatigue and anxiety. That may be why, when I look back on that protracted stay, it all feels the same: gray, rainy, chilly. Spring that year must have arrived with sunshine and daffodils. I was too gloomy to notice. But in all those long seven months, I never sensed that the weather was offering me a new start.

And what if I lived in the balmiest, steadiest, most soothing climate? When my husband and I visit Hawaii in midwinter, it feels—after icebound February in Minnesota—exactly like the paradise promised in tourist brochures. This blissful weather, we are assured by Hawaiian friends, never really changes. Of course this doesn't mean our friends don't experience mutations in their lives, but they don't happen to measure them by seasonal markers. How would I manage without those signals to take a breath, look around, and consider what might be next?

When I was young, I did not think about weather as a transforming force. I did not consciously think about weather much at all. It was simply part of my daily life, sometimes mildly bothersome—a canceled picnic or skating party—but never really troubling. Weather happened. That was all. Because we lived in town, and not on a farm, I never considered how a drought, or too much rain, or an early frost might have serious consequences. Now I know. I can no longer watch with pure exhilaration a January blizzard driving snow against my window, because I also picture a slow line of half-blinded drivers trying to make their way safely home. I look uneasily at brown cornfields in a record dry August and imagine the worried face of the farmer's wife in the farmhouse I am passing. I hear the heavily drumming rain with an uneasy suspicion that an old leak in our basement may be opening again. I think of drought, flood, whirlwinds, volcanic upheavals, tidal waves in other parts of the world.

I did not worry about the weather. I just listened to it. I now wonder if those childhood years of listening may have offered me another kind of transformation, a slow and gradual honing of my senses, a sharpened awareness of the world around me. Growing up in a Midwestern small town—unimaginably far from today's thudding tires, clanging horns, screeching sirens, roaring jet engines, blaring boom boxes, and tinkling cell phones—I was surrounded by quiet. The houses on our block might have been wrapped in invisible insulation. Surrounded by tall trees, shielded from the town's main highway by several intervening streets, people in our neighborhood—with their windows open—could never hear any other family's conversations or music or shouts or sobs.

But we could hear the weather. Insistent, unstoppable, it blew, dripped, clattered, crackled, and howled. Although it might be murmuring indecipherable messages, it forced its way into hearing. Nobody can make the weather quiet down. Most Midwesterners quickly learn to pay attention, and I did. This was undoubtedly useful. Since from an early age I was an avid reader, I easily disappeared into fantasy. Weather, among the other solid realities of my everyday life, helped to keep me from wandering too far. It constantly pulled me home. I began to notice what was there, what lay outside my window, what hovered in the very air I breathed.

So although I welcomed what our seasons could offer for fun— roasting marshmallows in a bonfire at our curb, falling backward into a high snowdrift, floating twig boats in an overflowing creek in spring, jumping from the highest springboard into a cold swimming pool on the hottest day of summer—I eventually began to appreciate our weather simply for what it was. I like to think of lying in my bed at night, just below a large window that looked out on our backyard. The yard was nothing special: a rectangle of grass, edged with trees and overgrown shrubs, patched with bits of garden. But the window let in the sounds of weather.

I loved listening to the rain. I have never truly believed it rains much in the Midwest. Oh, some years we have frequent storms and showers in May or June, maybe recurrent rain for some days in September or October. I know our flat farmland floods easily, and I've seen standing water in the fields. I am also aware that our creeks and rivers sometimes overflow their banks and cause ruinous trouble. But I can seldom get enough of it.

I slept at night so close to the window that I could hear the faintest light tapping of quick sharp drops, the kind of brief showery rain that passes through as quickly as a breeze. A soaking rain had a steady, rhythmic beat, deeply reassuring, the kind of sound that could soon lull me into sleep. When I was startled awake by the clap and crash of thunder, I would wait for another kind of rain, a frantic loud attack as if it were loosing a storm of metal arrows against the glass. Sitting up in bed, I quivered a little when a lightning flash gave me one quick glimpse of that pummeling rain, a moving curtain so thick I could scarcely see through it. Beyond that curtain lay something powerful, frightening—and eerily fascinating.

I think I loved the rain because it made everything else stop. Filling my ears, washing and soaking every surface, smearing and erasing what it touched, it blotted out my ordinary life. Rain flung glittering beads over my imagination, beckoning me into that mysterious place just beyond the dripping curtain. Lying there entranced, absorbing the music of rain on the window, rain on the shingles, rain on the grass, I found I could dissolve into half-waking dreams.

Of course I could not really hear the snow. But I sometimes thought I could. If I listened hard, really listened, I was sure I could catch the sound of all those thousands, millions, trillions of flakes falling everywhere in the backyard. I heard it as a soft and almost imperceptible sigh, a gentle exhaled breath, the lightest possible whisper. Only when a winter storm blew against my window did snow have a louder voice. Then the thick white flakes were nearly as brittle as glass, smashed by the wind as it whirled and tossed them into the trees, around the shrubs, over the buried garden. But when the storm ended, I knew I would discover a hushed white world whose silence was so deep I could disappear into it.

Sometimes I thought I could hear the heat too. On the hottest summer afternoons, if I slipped into my bedroom to lie on the bed and read, I could sense an audible quiver, a kind of faint vibrating, outside the window. Might it be the ground resisting, then giving way, as the heat rose and fell in attacking waves? Heavy and motionless, the air was on the verge of gasping for breath. Once I tried breaking an egg on our cement sidewalk, because a boy at school said the egg would sizzle as if it were in a frying pan on the stove. It didn't. It just lay at my feet in a yellow gluey mess. That didn't stop me from wondering if our cement driveway might soon begin to crack in the unrelenting heat, maybe with a slight but satisfying burble.

Through the year, all kinds of sounds drifted into my window, from the rustle of blowing leaves in the fall to the uneven drip of melting icicles in the spring sunshine. But different as they were, most voices of the weather arrived on the wind. Anyone who has grown up in the Midwest knows about wind. It seems to be blowing all the time. On dead-quiet summer days, the complete absence of wind makes the gloating heat more ominous, as if somewhere, on the edge of this miasma, the wind is sucking in its breath to gather a black storm that can fill the void.

Our wind blows in soft tickles, short brisk puffs, and shrill witch calls. It can be hot or cold, loud or soft, light or heavy. It pokes, flaps, and bristles. Probing into the most unlikely recesses, it can murmur enticing promises or threaten chaos and destruction. No one can tell when it will start or stop. Sometimes I notice the wind only because, kneeling in the garden, I see the wispy down on a nearby dandelion seed head beginning to dance a little. Other times the wind is so loud, pounding hard, shaking windows, slamming garbage cans and flower-pots, that it drowns out all other noise. Those who have been far too close to a tornado often describe its sound as a screaming locomotive, a train barreling down upon them with clacketing wheels and shrieking whistle.

Midwesterners grow up aware that their wind blows from beyond the western mountains or northern tundras, speeding past prairie, fields, low hills, lakes, and river valleys, picking up dust or rain or snow on its way. It may pour straight down upon us or circle in meandering detours. Hearing the wind, if I take the time to listen closely, I can easily imagine it as a traveler with irresistible tales to tell.

When I hear the wind in most large cities, it does not sound the same. The wind feels cramped, cross, distracted. Its muffled voice turns harsh because it has to battle with so many others. So it slams doors, flaps at windows, and clangs garbage cans. Making its way among buildings, blockades, and narrow streets, the wind sometimes nearly loses its power of speech. Instead, flexing a little muscle, it has to show what it can do. In London or New York, I notice the wind mostly by its antics—its petulant tugs at umbrellas, its whirling pounces on loose bits of paper, its mischievous lifting of skirts and unanchored hats. Vigorous as it can be, the wind in a large city is somehow diminished.

Growing up in the Midwest, I gradually developed a kind of tuning apparatus, like a delicately balanced sounding fork, that resonates with the weather. That may be partly a natural instinct for survival, since anyone who does not pay attention to severe heat, subzero cold, looming thunderstorms, or sudden blizzards would soon be in trouble. But our weather has also brought me a heightened awareness of the world beyond my protective walls, a world full of mutating possibilities. As the weather shifts, I can sense a movement, a potential change, in myself. Sometimes I find this unwelcome, even disturbing. But, in a more complicated way than when I was young, I often feel that the weather is full of promise.

# Other Weather, Other Places

There'll be a change in the weather, a change in the sea,
Before long there'll be a change in me.

> —Billy Higgins and W. Benton Overstreet,
> "There'll Be Some Changes Made"

I DO NOT ALWAYS FEEL PLEASED or excited by Midwest weather. I don't even like it all the time. Sometimes, in fact, I hate it. Then I want to flee—now! this moment! Since my imagination can travel far and fast, I have stored a number of possible escapes in a phantasmal Pandora's box. On some July mornings, heavy and stifling as wet wool, I think longingly of Mendocino, a four-hour drive north of San Francisco. I also think of Mendocino in midwinter as I stare out the window at newly gleaming ice and wonder if I dare try a sliding walk around the lake. Mendocino is one of my Other Places, where, on difficult days, I am convinced I ought to live.

It is probably cloudy this morning on the Northern California coast. A faint foggy haze hovers over the sea, except for momentary gleams when slanting rays of sun slash through the gray. I know how the pools of water in the rocky coves would then briefly turn a translucent blue-green. I would need a light jacket on a morning like this, something I could later tie around my waist when the sun gets stronger, and maybe a hat to pull over my ears. It would be a good morning to walk, or drink tea, or place my laptop in front of a window and begin to write. Just for today—and maybe tomorrow—I would like to live in Mendocino weather.

Throughout my fifty-plus years in the Midwest, I have often needed somewhere else to fantasize about. Perhaps I picture myself living in other places, other weather, because I had not planned to end up here. Although I was happy as a child in Iowa in the 1940s and 1950s, I assumed that I would eventually leave one day, never to return. I loved Ames, but I dreamed of ruined castles, ancient woods, dark London garrets, flowery meadows, towering mountains, turbulent seas—all the surroundings Iowa didn't have.

I wasn't quite sure where I would want to live, but by the time I was in high school, I had begun to consider various possibilities. By then I had absorbed almost every Technicolor musical ever made, and I thought I knew something of New York *(Silk Stockings, Lullaby of Broadway, On the Town)*, London *(Royal Wedding)*, and Paris *(An American in Paris, Gigi, Funny Face)*. Flowery parks, horse-drawn hansom cabs, sidewalk cafés, skyscrapers, the Seine, Buckingham Palace, moorlands, the Eiffel Tower: all glittered on my horizon.

Considering where I would someday live, I did not give any thought to weather. And although I heard my mother's friends complain about Ames, these cosmopolitan grown-ups never singled out weather as Iowa's greatest flaw. They had other grievances. Mrs. Keller, a gourmet cook who had lived in California, once summed up her lingering disappointment in Ames in one damning sentence: "You can't buy any good cheese here."

When I eventually attended college in Massachusetts, the seasons were not drastically different from Iowa's. Spring was a little earlier, fall more attention-getting, winter less frigid. But when I arrived in Berkeley, California, for graduate school, I was astonished. Each morning, I woke to fresh delight. The weather was perfect: never too hot, never too cold. Of course it rained sometimes, but the rain didn't bother me. I liked to hear it pattering on the window, singing me into sleep, or nudging me gently but firmly to a cozy carrel in the library.

Mostly I remember light breeze, a certain briskness in the air, and, surprisingly—given the annual rainfall—sunshine. When I stood on the steps of International House, the graduate-student residence where I lived, I could look across the bay to San Francisco. Some mornings fog hid everything. But at the right time of day, the sun could strike the pastel houses of the city, turning them into a distant Moorish fairy tale. The orange girders of the Golden Gate then became a gilded arch over the sea. On the far side of the arch was Marin County. My favorite radio station often punctuated its breaks with an announcer chanting soulfully, "And the dusk is falling over Marin, while the fog rolls in over the Golden Gate Bridge."

For my whole first semester, I had a hard time concentrating on my studies. When days dawned like this in Iowa, everyone more or less agreed, "How could we possibly work today?" Each Berkeley day offered new possibilities, a kind of temperate assurance that anything would work out fine. I could do what I wanted, be what I wanted. When I explored, with timorous wonder, the topsy-turvy streets of San Francisco, I walked in a new pair of black leather thonged sandals, handcrafted by a longhaired shoemaker on Berkeley's funky Telegraph Avenue. My khaki trench coat was loosely belted, determinedly casual, yet ready for action. I felt rather like a foreign correspondent, which, in a way, I was.

When I married Lawrence, my first husband, we left Berkeley after a year. He took a teaching position at the University of Minnesota, and I packed my trench coat and sandals. I didn't need them much after that. Nobody wore sandals like mine in Minneapolis, and my trench coat was either too heavy or not warm enough. I had my first insight into what was waiting when Lawrence and I flew to Minneapolis for his interview. The department chairman wanted to meet me, too. It was early February, and Berkeley, as we drove away from our apartment, was newly green, bursting with flowers and riotous shrubs.

In Minneapolis, no fresh snow had fallen for some time. Blackened mounds that might have harbored ice rats lurked in dark corners and alleys. Bits of litter were emerging damply from thawing ice. On Saturday night, as we waited in a long line for a movie we'd already seen in San Francisco, I watched as an icy wind tumbled crumpled paper, gum wrappers, and cigarette foil down Hennepin Avenue, deserted except for our straggling line. It would take me years in Minnesota to learn to wait patiently while the bleakest part of February passed by.

That first year in Minneapolis, I learned that weather did matter. Maybe because my new marriage wasn't easy, I remember that winter of 1965 with grim clarity. For Minnesota, I don't think it was especially cold, unusually snowy, or remarkable in any way. But I found it hard. For the past three years, I had been used to grabbing a light wrap and hurrying out the door. Now I had to prepare carefully for every excursion. Sleet, snow, windchill that might zoom to forty or fifty below zero—this took more than a hasty swipe at the closet. Since I felt I had a certain tenuous position as a young faculty wife, I couldn't look too kooky, or informal, or sloppy. But somehow I had to try to keep warm. Despite my best efforts, I could never get properly suited up.

When I think of that first winter, I immediately picture the mall on the University of Minnesota campus on a dark, snowy, fearsomely cold Friday night. That was the night we went to "the symphony"— shorthand, then, for the weekly concerts of the Minneapolis Symphony. Both Lawrence and I liked classical music, and I had told myself before marriage that this was one of our important common interests. We had to work on those. Soon after we moved to Minneapolis, I made sure we bought season tickets. I had not quite realized that, since I was a graduate student again, I might be tired at the end of a long week of classes.

Nor had I realized how long a walk it was in the cold from the parking lot a few blocks away, where Lawrence fortunately had an on-campus space, down the mall to Northrop Auditorium, where the orchestra performed. I wince when I remember my flimsy dresses and nylon stockings. How else could I feel appropriate? Who (in the mid 1960s) would have considered wearing slacks to a concert? For I was not unusual; most of the women I saw at the symphony wore, under their furs or sheepskins or heavy tweed coats, the kind of dressy outfits seen at church, or weddings, or important dinner parties.

In winter, driving to the symphony was often an adventure. For a wedding present, Lawrence's affluent and generous parents had given us a red Porsche 356B convertible, a small sleek car that fitted seamlessly into the Berkeley landscape. Its black top rolled down, it soared with aplomb up and down the steep Berkeley and San Francisco hills. But it was not at home in Minnesota. Chill seeped past its thickly padded canvas roof as easily as through a summer screen. On ice, our road-hugging Porsche no longer seemed sure of itself. Lawrence, who stubbornly clung to the idea that our life in Minnesota need not be so different, valiantly insisted, however, that his beloved Porsche was wonderful in snow.

On winter Friday nights, we often put this belief to the test. One Friday, the snow began gently falling at noon. The sky was lowering and dark in midafternoon. The snow kept falling, thicker and thicker. By the time Lawrence came home at suppertime, white drifts had buried our sidewalk and alley. But the city's indomitable snowplows, clanking and roaring, were already chewing up the snow on some of the streets. "It's bad out there," Lawrence said, "but we're going." Last Friday we had missed the symphony because I had a migraine; something unsaid—lost money, my failings, our future in Minnesota—was suddenly at stake.

Because so many stalled commuters' cars were clogging traffic on the main roads, Lawrence decided we would have to take back streets through residential neighborhoods. Once we started, Lawrence didn't say much. He gripped the steering wheel with a kind of fervor I was beginning to know well. "Hold *on!*" he might warn, as we slid toward a curb, or *"Okay!"* as we recovered and managed to careen around a corner. He did not dare to stop at most stop signs—fortunately, almost no one else was out driving that night—since we might not have been able to scrape up enough traction to lurch forward again. On we went, bumping through the white-fogged, deserted streets, veering and zigzagging, trying to decipher the faint tire tracks crunched down by earlier cars. I clutched the edges of my bucket seat. If we slammed into a snowbank, I did not know what would happen. Could we push ourselves out? Would we miss the whole concert? And then what?

We thudded into Lawrence's parking lot, crashing through a low drift barring its entrance, minutes before the concert was scheduled to begin. I took a deep breath as I opened the car door into the frozen dark. Inside, the car felt warm from its seven-mile drive. The auditorium looked impossibly far away. As I bolted down the long mall, the wind pounced, whistling up my short skirt. Frostbite was sinking its teeth into my shrinking flesh. By the time I thankfully opened the auditorium door and nearly fell into the blast of overheated air, I was numb everywhere. Then, warming up, moments after I collapsed into my seat, I began to drift into an exhausted sleep. I had to fight, over and over again, to stay awake.

Long months later, summer arrived. It was very humid and very hot. Our second-floor duplex was not air-conditioned, and I often tried to find some breeze by escaping to a small screened porch that opened off our bedroom. When I think of that first Minnesota summer, I remember my piano stool. Longing for music in my life, without having to brave the weather, I had bought myself an old upright piano. Since it came without a bench, I had decided to equip it instead with an adjustable, claw-footed piano stool. Knowing I had to watch our budget carefully—I was a student, earning nothing—I decided to buy a battered Victorian stool from a local junk shop and refinish it myself. The man at the hardware store, smoothly assembling paint remover, sandpaper, tack cloth, brushes, turpentine, stain, and glossy varnish, said this would be easy.

When I see myself on those steamy sunny afternoons, crouched on a layer of newspapers spread over the porch boards, I almost begin to sweat again. Hour after hour, while the sun baked the asbestos porch roof and poked searchingly into my shifting shadows of half shade, I sanded, rubbed, and edged carefully around knobs and curlicues. Old varnish clung stubbornly to every convoluted inch. The sharp, searing odor of stripper, turpentine, and stain hung in the still air. I do not remember any breeze at all. From the porch I looked out onto a narrow, scrubby backyard, whose browned crabgrass and wilting dandelions were barely surviving a midsummer drought. At the end of the yard I could see a drooping, straggling line of hollyhocks against the garage and trash can.

I had an epiphany at that trash can. Our garbage was collected once a week, and just after the last pickup, Lawrence and I had finally finished most of a watermelon. I decided to throw the rest out. Since our landlady lined the trash can with a plastic bag, I didn't bother to wrap the hacked-up hunk of watermelon. I dumped it into the empty trash can and forgot about it. Days later, I carried more garbage outside. When I lifted the trash can lid, I gasped. Our discarded watermelon, no longer pale red and green, was now mostly white. More alarming, it was alive. Swarming over the melon were hundreds of tiny white maggots. Staring down, and watching them scurry with blind avidity over the rotting carcass, I wondered where they had come from. Had they been conjured by the malevolent heat out of the soggy atmosphere? Did they hibernate in winter and then emerge, secretly and silently, to multiply with every breath of summer? Where—and just how near—had they been waiting?

I had never seen maggots in Berkeley. During my first arduous year in Minneapolis, I thought often of Northern California, which now seemed like a lost paradise, evergreen and cool. Although I slowly began to settle back into the Midwest, I kept an idealized image of the Bay Area as a place where life was easier, more joyful, more productive. When I heard news from a few graduate school friends who lingered there, I persuaded myself, despite hearing of their problems—stalled theses, scarce jobs, troubled love affairs, struggling marriages—that they *had* to be happier than I was. Didn't they live in a place where, each morning, they could wake up and know the weather, the very air, would welcome them?

Summer passed, fall whirled by, and it was soon winter again. As season followed season, I slowly began to think of myself as a true Minnesotan. During my second winter, I bought shiny new ice skates, and soon I learned, waveringly but determinedly, to cross-country ski, at least on nearly level ground. As soon as we owned a house with a backyard, I rushed outside to my garden in early spring, just as soon as I could work the rich black Midwestern soil. On hot summer afternoons, I drove to a nearby outdoor swimming pool for "adult lap hour" and sometimes paddled on my back, splashing cold water, looking up with pleasure at the radiant blue sky. In fall I biked along the high banks of the Mississippi River, admiring the gold, yellow, and russet leaves that framed the gleaming water far below. Like most Minnesotans, I talked a lot about the weather. I was rather proud that we had more of it than anywhere else.

But at difficult times, I flashed back to Northern California. It was impossible for me to return. I was married, my husband had a job in Minnesota, and eventually, after completing my Ph.D., I did too. By the 1970s, academic positions in college English departments were hard to find, and I knew I was lucky. But when my life felt burdensome, I would picture myself in San Francisco. Gradually I developed a kind of alternate existence there, a dream self who now lived in a sunlit apartment on a San Francisco hill. I was teaching somewhere, maybe at San Francisco State, where I'd actually had a part-time post for a year before Lawrence and I had left California.

Before long, I could see my life in San Francisco clearly. My one-bedroom apartment was just the right size for me, a snuggly calico cat, and a few chosen friends who came for brunch. My rooms had polished wood floors, which set off billowy white curtains. In a wrought iron window box I kept pots of bright red and pink geraniums, exuberantly spilling over the railings.

Of course I'd meet someone. My husband and I, idyllically happy, would move to Marin, or maybe to a houseboat in Sausalito. But somehow, beyond our move, I could never quite continue to picture this new life. I could only get as far as cat, geraniums, and houseboat. Then my imagination failed. It was overwhelmed by the marriage I already had.

I clung to these far-off visions for most of the eleven years of my marriage, although, grounded as I had become in the reality of the Midwest, I slowly had to admit to myself that this other life was indeed a fantasy. If I had once had a chance to alight in that flower-bedecked apartment, I had long since lost it. Weeds—thick, impenetrable, thorny—had grown over the road not taken.

Eventually I stopped seeing myself in other places, other weather. After my daughter, Jennifer, was born, I was so enraptured—and stunned into exhaustion—that I could not picture any life beyond her next feeding. Or beyond her current cold, or first steps, or the opening of kindergarten. But when, at thirty-four, I found myself divorced, living alone, and supporting a three-year-old child, I felt restless again. I began to wonder once more about other possibilities in life. At the moment, I didn't have any. I was teaching full time, and when I rushed home, I was unpacking groceries, cooking, cleaning, paying bills, and trying not to snap at Jennifer when she persisted in asking why I didn't want to sit on the living room floor and play Snakes and Ladders or Uncle Wiggly.

Midwestern weather is not friendly to mothers with small children. Once I heard an apocryphal story, passed from one young mother to another, that I wryly recalled on the first cold winter day. "This mother, I think she was a friend of my friend Julie's, or Barbara's," the story went, "had just moved to Minnesota from North Carolina. Or maybe it was Florida, or California. Anyway, she had just moved here with her three children, all under the age of five. Of course she went right down to Dayton's and bought them new snowsuits and mittens and boots. Scarves, too, I suppose. Maybe little muffs for the girls.

"On the first really cold day, she took all this stuff out of the closet and started to bundle her kids up, one by one. It took a long time, because you know how it is, trying to stuff squirmy kids into those zip-up snowsuits and then wangle their feet into bulky boots. Their mittens kept falling off, and their scarves came unwound. But after about half an hour, she finally had everyone ready. The car was warmed up. They were a little late, and just as she started herding the kids to the door, the smallest one pulled at her sleeve and said, 'Mommy! Mommy! Wait! I have to go potty!' Well, this mother just sat down on the floor and cried."

I loved this story. Even when Jennifer was old enough to insist on choosing (and maybe not bothering to fasten) her own jacket, I thought of it occasionally as I struggled to pull on my own stubborn leg-hugging boots. I understood the energy, the planning, the foresight that this young mother had invested in preparing for winter. She was determined to cope. Weren't we all? But most of all, I loved how she finally just gave up and cried. Sometimes that was all anyone could do.

So, a few years after my divorce, I began to dream again of an easier, more manageable life—and, yes, of better weather. What if I moved back to San Francisco? What might I do there now? I was frequently weary of murky student prose, tedious arguments about grades, interminable committee meetings. One afternoon, as our daughters played together, I confided my complaints to a close friend who also taught at my college. She nodded at everything I said.

"I know what I want to do, and one of these days I'm going to do it," Emily said firmly. "I'm going to open a shop that sells stuffed animals. Just stuffed animals. I've already picked out the huge giraffe I'll have at the front, by the window." She described the layout of the store, just where it would be, the hours it would be open.

That, I assured her eagerly, was a great idea. I had thought of something like that too! Well, not stuffed animals, but jade. I had loved jade jewelry ever since I'd seen apple-green bangle bracelets, multicolor clustered rings, and long pale green necklaces in Gump's, the store that in the 1960s had symbolized for me all of San Francisco's glamour. After Emily and I giggled together over our plans— though she insisted she was quite serious, and I told her that really, I was too—I began to think more about this tempting idea.

To open a jade shop in Minneapolis, I needed to know more. I'd have to learn all about jade. So that would be why I'd have to move back to San Francisco! I would apprentice myself to the jade buyer at Gump's! Then I'd study Chinese, so I could travel to the Orient on buying trips. Northwest Airlines then had a haunting signature tune, "Northwest Oh-ree-ent Airlines," accented with the gentle chime of temple bells.

Although I'd return to Minneapolis eventually to open my shop, for a few years I could find that San Francisco apartment after all— bigger, now that I had Jennifer. Actually, when I got to this point in my fantasy, I stopped cold. What about Jennifer? What would she be doing on those evenings I was studying Chinese? Where would she stay while I was visiting China?

So I never wrote to Gump's, and Emily, as far as I know, never inquired about rents on St. Paul's Grand Avenue. But whenever academic life felt stifling, I clung to this possibility, seeing myself hiking on a Sunday afternoon in Muir Woods, sipping Irish coffee with a friend at the Buena Vista café, pausing in my car to watch a sunset on Ocean Beach. The weather in my daydreams was perfect.

For years, San Francisco was my Other Place. Eventually, however, it faded. After all, I now had tenure, and—the goal of most academics—I was finally a full professor. I added new insulation to my old house in St. Paul. I bought an air conditioner for the bedroom. I dug a bigger hole in the middle of my backyard lawn for an expanded garden. Then, when I was forty-four, and Jenny thirteen, I married James and moved from St. Paul to his house near Lake Harriet in Minneapolis. I enjoyed living just steps away from a beautiful lake, and I felt blissful about my marriage. What more could I want?

Except I still needed an Other Place. One March, when the Midwest's lingering winter dribbled bits of snow like disheartened stains on the brown grass, I joined James on a quick business trip to San Francisco. Afterward, we took three days to drive north to a town I'd found on the map. I wanted a long vista of ocean, I told James, and Mendocino looked like just the spot to find it. It was. Instantly I longed for a house on the sea in Mendocino. I wanted to be near the winding path along the headlands at the edge of the sea; the endless deserted beach a few miles north of Fort Bragg; the tangy smell of a redwood forest in the damp early morning. What a place to write! What a place to live! What energizing, salt-breeze weather!

But James was deeply rooted in Minneapolis. His family, his architectural office, his teaching position—none could be transplanted. And I had happily grafted my life onto his. We might frequently return to Mendocino for vacations, and we did, but we could never live there. "Well," James once said cheerfully, "if I predecease you, you can sell up and move to Mendocino." I would sometimes try to ponder this, rather as I used to picture a single life in San Francisco, but all my images now looked far too lonely.

For several years, I pretended that if the inconceivable happened, I might indeed leave the Midwest, where I had now lived most of my life, and head for Mendocino. What would I do there? I might volunteer somewhere, I could work a few afternoons in one of the shops, and I would write. What about a novel? I started to outline a vague plot, involving a young widow (much younger than I, not me at all, I told myself) who fled to Mendocino to start a new life. She might arrive just for a few months' stay. Maybe she could offer to run a bed-and-breakfast inn for old friends who had an unspecified emergency? At any rate, she wouldn't necessarily be planning to stay.

And then, not too long after arriving, on a walk just after dawn along the headlands, she might stop, for no particular reason, and peer down over the unprotected edge of a cliff. Far, far below, in a little cove, she would see a circle of sand. Lying facedown on this tiny inaccessible beach was a body. An older woman, I thought, in a long coat. I didn't know who the woman was yet, though I knew someone had pushed her over. She had no identification in her pockets, and no one in Mendocino had seen her before. Well, almost no one. I could work on several likely suspects among the villagers.

One suspect was the veterinarian. Because of course I needed a love interest, and my widow had already begun to fall a little in love with the local veterinarian. His name was Mike. Or Doug, or Pete. Tweedy, kind, a twinkle in his eye. (Or was he shy and serious?) But this is where I blanked. Just as, years before, I'd stalled at how I might arrange proper care for my young daughter in San Francisco while I myself merrily tripped off to China, I couldn't get past the veterinarian.

The problem was that I knew nothing about vets, and, if I were honest, not all that much about men's inner lives. So I'd have to find a Mike, or Doug, or Pete, and ask if I could unobtrusively hang around for a while, days or maybe weeks. I'd have to hover in an operating room, observe sick dogs and frightened cats, watch probing or incisions or terminal injections. Not only didn't I want to spend any time with this vet, but I was convinced that even if I did, I would never really understand him. So my plot languished. I already knew, though, how my story had to end. The widow would return to Minneapolis.

I wouldn't close the door completely. Maybe she would write a bittersweet letter to Doug (or Pete, or Mike), holding out the hope of her coming back to Mendocino. But for now, she wanted to go home. I wasn't entirely sure why. Did she miss her friends? Or family? I wasn't sure. Or did she just want to be there before the first snow fell, so she could watch the thick white flakes falling softly outside her window?

These days I don't think much about Mendocino. Not long ago, after I had published a laudatory travel essay about the Northern California coast, I had a letter from an old acquaintance. "I read your piece with interest," Marnie wrote. "But you need to know that life out there isn't perfect either. My married daughter Amy lives just outside Mendocino, and she gets antsy in such a small community, so remote and enclosed, and so far from any major airport. Besides, I think you'd find that those long gray months, with so much rain and not much sun, would get to you. They sure get to Amy."

So there it was: the weather again. In Berkeley, another friend tells me, a polluting miasma often hangs over the bay. It's not much like the place I once knew, he adds. So, I think a little sadly, summers there are probably duller, winters rainier, and the sun doesn't shine as much as I remember. Maybe it never did. First Berkeley and San Francisco, then Mendocino: maybe I am ready to give up my dream of an Other Place.

One Other Place—the island that encompasses England, Scotland, and Wales—has a special niche in my life. I love that island (and its outlying islands), and I revisit as often as I can. Since I write so affectionately about Britain, many readers assume that I must long to move there. Some send me letters with helpful suggestions about how I could, and once, several years ago, another reader who urged me publicly to take the next flight made me think about why I don't. This reader was on the staff of a local tabloid, now defunct, the kind distributed free in coffee shops and lobbies. The paper used to run a popular annual feature called "Get Out of Town." Its contributing writers were invited to compose vituperative short essays, nominating people they particularly disliked and wanted to see leave the Twin Cities, and the paper gleefully published all the essays. One year a former student from the college where I'd taught seized his opportunity and nominated me. Why, he fumed, after a zestful attack, since I loved England so much, didn't I just do Minneapolis a favor and move there?

Although his tone was mean, his question was actually quite perceptive. I did once think I might want to move to London, or Cornwall, or an island in the Hebrides. For many years after my first trip to Britain in 1960, I thought of England—or Scotland or Wales—as the farthest fantasy of my Other Places. As if willing myself to enter a fairy tale, I tried to create an imaginary life in a thatch-roofed cottage along a Dorset lane, or a snug gray-stone cottage on a wind-lashed Scottish coast, or a half-timbered Tudor house in a small Welsh town. On trips to Britain, I'd rush to buy copies of *Country Life,* its oversized pages filled with dazzling full-color advertisements for impossibly expensive country houses. I would carefully study them, trying to decide which one I wanted most (because I wanted them all). Sometimes I put myself into an imposing historic mansion with nine bedrooms, stables, and a lodge, set in a garden designed by Gertrude Jekyll and surrounded by a deer park with lake; other times I settled for a Regency mews apartment in Kensington; in modest moments I chose a restored barn nestled into the Sussex Downs.

But I changed my mind. In 1978, I spent seven months living in London with Jenny, a chapter I called "A Shady Patch" in *My Love Affair with England,* because that time felt so dark. Dark, cold, and damp. That winter was a particularly harsh one in England, and, feeling overworked and lonely, I remember lying at night on my lumpy bed, encased in down-filled bathrobe and covered with blankets, desperately trying to keep warm. Although I now relish the cool, gray days of an English spring, I remember how I longed then for a liberating wash of bright blue sky.

In recent years, I've been lucky enough to travel to Britain often. When I'm not there, I miss it. But that does not mean I want to move.

I know that my misgivings about weather there are surprisingly important. They remind me, among other things, that I am undeniably American. I have been shaped by a loud, brash, show-offy climate, a Midwest that echoes with thunderclaps, howls with windstorms, piles up its snowdrifts with abandon, and noisily drenches its fields with floods. That is part of who I am, a woman apt to erupt in unrestrained chortling laughter, fond of reds and purples, unexpectedly emotional, often given to sweeping gestures. Here, not England—at least for now—is where I belong.

Last winter, as I walked one icy morning with a friend, we were complaining about having to watch each step. "Do you ever think about moving somewhere south, like New Mexico or Arizona, when you get a lot older?" she asked me. "So you don't have to worry about falling?" I laughed. That morning I was nursing a wrenched shoulder. The night before, I had tripped on an errant slipper in our bedroom and fallen so ungracefully that, despite landing on a soft carpet, I knew my shoulder would hurt for days. I would have fallen just as hard in Arizona.

"I might miss this," I said, gesturing with a mittened hand over the lake. The cold wind had burnished the cloudless blue sky, and the sun shone so brilliantly on the snow-covered lake that its whiteness almost burned through my sunglasses. The air had the piercing clarity of a metal whistle. When I got home, I'd unpeel all my layers of clothing and fix myself a cup of hot chocolate. It would be a good afternoon to sit on the sofa and read a little before getting back to work. At least for now, I would not think longingly of any other place, or any other weather.

# Storms

"I don't like it," Pa said, slowly shaking his head. "I don't like the feel of the weather. There's something . . ." He could not say what he meant and he said again, "I don't like it. I don't like it at all."

—Laura Ingalls Wilder, *The Long Winter*

ALL YEAR VIOLENT STORMS can sweep over the Midwest, sudden onslaughts of thunder and lightning, wind, rain, snow, sleet, hail. But I remember one particular storm as if it has compressed all the others into a single mesmerizing hour. When I think about my first marriage—what went wrong and why I left—I keep coming back to a late afternoon in June. I did not recognize what was happening until many years later. But I think I passed a landmark, a point of no return, during this summer storm.

"When the funnel hits, we'll have to crawl out a window," I remember Lawrence telling me with high-pitched firmness. "Probably that one." He pointed to a narrow slit of glass high on the basement wall. I stared at it, wondering how I would get up and through it. Climb on a chair? The window might be just large enough, I thought, unless I got caught on shards of glass. "We'll break it if we have to," he went on, "and then head for the garage. If it's standing."

The wind howled, our small house shook, and I was sure that at any moment the walls would begin to crumple. Although it was only four o'clock, the sky was so dark that it felt like night. Rain slashed sideways against the blinded windows. I could not imagine myself outside in this whirlwind of water. Through the window, I repeated to myself, then race to the garage. What would happen during that frantic dash? Would one of our trees smash across my path?

No one in the Twin Cities had expected a storm that afternoon. We had taken our small collapsible sailboat to White Bear Lake, north of St. Paul, and spent a quiet sun-baked afternoon on the water. After we came home, we carefully unloaded the lightweight boat from the top of our car and carried it to its sawhorses in the backyard. Perhaps an hour later, I went outside again. The air indoors had grown very still, the sky had begun to darken, and I wanted to check the sky. What I saw looked ominous. Not far in the west the horizon had turned a strange yellow-greenish color. Boiling storm clouds were moving toward us with astonishing speed. As I watched, they began to cross the Mississippi River, only two blocks away. I yelled for Lawrence.

He came running out. After one quick glance at the sky, he cried, "The boat! Come on, we have to get it behind the garage!" Between one side of the garage and the steep slope that separated us from our neighbors was a narrow level space, heaped with leaves and bits of junk, but just wide enough for the Klepper. Each of us grabbed an end and trotted clumsily across the yard with the boat. Together we dumped the boat and ran back toward the house. Already the clouds were almost overhead, and a sudden powerful wind had bent the trees.

"The cats!" I called out. "You get Humphrey, I'll find Paprika! Bring them down to the basement!" We ran for the house. With one vicious blast, the wind slammed the door shut as soon as I had opened it. We both rushed through several rooms until we had found our Siamese cats and carried them, meowing and struggling, down the stairs. They began to prowl the basement floor, talking and complaining, but I felt unable to move. Although I wondered if I should dash back upstairs to rescue anything else—my dissertation notes? my jewelry?—I could hear the wind howling louder and louder. So I hunched myself into the southwest corner, where I could look up at a small high window.

The southwest corner was a critical spot. When a tornado approaches, Midwestern radio and television announcers interrupt their programming with loud peremptory blasts and staccato warnings. For years, they cautioned everyone to seek immediate shelter in the southwest corner of their basements. (Now we are supposed to hunker down in various other protected places, including, bizarrely, a bathtub.) For some reason, storms usually strike from a direction that would presumably leave this corner relatively unscathed. The best position, metaphorically and physically, was flat against the cement-block wall. Waiting for the house overhead to blow away, one can feel the force of the clichés "backed into a corner" and "up against the wall."

The high window, our only spyhole, was bleared and dirty. Now, with the rain falling, we could see almost nothing. "I'll check out what's going on," Lawrence said, as he headed eagerly back up the basement stairs. Lawrence loved a crisis. In some ways he was at his most imaginative and resourceful then, because he expected the worst and began to prepare for it. He could, and did, somersault ahead to all the implications of an impending disaster.

I remember the first time in our marriage when he announced that something quite awful was about to happen. We were on our honeymoon in Europe, just a few days after arriving and picking up our new Porsche at the Stuttgart factory. One afternoon Lawrence noticed a slight clacking sound somewhere in the car. It grew worse at certain speeds. He could not locate the source of this metallic flutter, and he grew increasingly concerned. His face tightened; his voice became sharp. Recognizing these storm signs, I anxiously studied our handbook of authorized Porsche service until I found a garage thirty or forty miles farther.

As we drove on, with a noise that now had become a threatening rat-a-tat-tat, Lawrence began to warn me about what to expect. "Forget about the rest of the honeymoon," he said, looking straight ahead. His voice was very angry. "We'll have to turn around and drive this back to Stuttgart. They've clearly sold us a defective car." He paused, then added in a rush, "By the time we get a new one, and I'm not sure I want one now, we'll have wasted so much time there would be no point in going on. We'll take the next plane home." He gripped the steering wheel more tightly and added defiantly, "And as soon as we get home, we'll have to sue."

When we finally pulled into the Porsche-certified garage, Lawrence, who spoke German, jumped out of the car and began to talk with a mechanic. I could not understand what they were saying. Moments later, Lawrence motioned me out of the car. He and the mechanic got in, and they sped off together. As I loitered uneasily on the cement forecourt, I thought ahead to our trip back to Stuttgart. Then I painfully reviewed our ruined itinerary—farewell to Austria, Switzerland, Holland—and wondered glumly how I'd be able to cancel all our reservations.

When Lawrence and the mechanic returned, the mechanic got out, smiled, and said something genial in German as he walked away. Lawrence hopped back into the driver's seat and said to me, "Get in." I did, very quickly. I could tell he didn't feel like talking. But as we drove away, I said nervously, "Well? What is it? What's happened?" Since I knew nothing about cars, I could not guess.

Lawrence drove in silence for a few moments and then gave a kind of sour laugh. "It's the heater flaps," he said. I was puzzled. I knew the car's heat came from small outlets near the back seats, and those outlets had sliding flaplike metal doors. But we hadn't needed any heat. What did heat have to do with anything? "We didn't have the flaps fully closed," Lawrence went on reluctantly. "So that's what was making the rattle. They're metal. They were vibrating." The heater flaps—and the subject—were now firmly closed, but, I realized with relief, our honeymoon was still on.

So, huddled in the southwest corner of our basement, I should have known that Lawrence wasn't necessarily right. The worst might not happen. The problem was that I found this extraordinarily hard to believe. As a psychologist once told me, anyone who loses a parent in early life—I was seven when my father died—tends to see the world as an uncertain place, liable at any moment to unforeseen disasters. So when Lawrence, highly intelligent and instantly ready with strong opinions, said with assurance that the sky was falling, I was easily convinced that it was.

The sky did seem to be falling in Minnesota that June afternoon, smashing against our house and everything around it. "What about the boat?" I quavered. We had stretched our budget to buy the Klepper. I thought of it lying on a heap of rotten leaves, unprotected except for the lee of the small garage. "Destroyed by now," Lawrence answered without hesitation. "All it would take is one big branch coming down on top of it. Or anything else, with the force of that wind. Listen to how things are blowing around out there." I listened.

In minutes, the power went out. Just across the street from our front yard was a tall electricity pole with a transformer. Soon I heard a deafening crack, loud enough to be heard over the screaming wind. Then, reflected in our rain-smeared windows, I could see frightening spurts of light, as if fires were splashing into our yard. Lawrence sprinted upstairs and down again. "That's the transformer," he reported. "The live wires are thrashing back and forth on the ground. They'll probably whip across the street to your car." I parked my old Volvo in front of the house. "So get ready," Lawrence went on, with a grim zest, "because the next sound you hear will be your car exploding."

I cannot remember exactly how long the storm lasted. At its height, when Lawrence began to plan our escape, I thought it might go on for hours. I wished I didn't know what tornadoes could do. I kept remembering my beloved Aunt Ted. As I cowered against the cement-block wall, I recalled the 1957 tornado that hit Fargo, North Dakota. Although I respectfully thought of it as "Aunt Ted's tornado," the tornado, far from being a personal attack on my aunt, had devastated whole sections of the city.

Like all my mother's family, Aunt Ted, whose nickname was an unlikely variant of Theresa, had a strong will. When she and Mother disagreed about something, usually politics, I could almost hear their clashes as a muted clanging in the air. Although my mother, when she was infuriated or deeply wounded, would sometimes begin to cry,

Aunt Ted didn't. So I thought of her as unusually tough. That is why I cherished the image of her during the Fargo tornado.

Soon afterward, my mother, reading a letter from Ted, described the terrible wind and rain and then, as the tornado approached, a sound like a freight train bearing down on the house. My uncle and two cousins ran for the basement. But, said Mother with an admiring shake of her head, Ted didn't want to abandon her house. Her living room, her dining room table and chairs, all her valued possessions—how could she let them go? So, as I heard the story, my uncle had to run back up the stairs. There he found Aunt Ted, her legs braced, trying to hold the front door against the wind.

Nothing too disastrous happened. Aunt Ted was persuaded to join the rest of the family in the basement. The tornado tore into a house three doors south; another house, even closer, lost its roof as if sliced by a knife. Aunt Ted's family emerged from the basement to find their roof damaged but still attached, though all their windows had been blown out. My cousin Jim remembers his surprise on finding a brick lying in the upstairs hallway and a cedar board on top of his bed. Not long ago, when I asked him about his memories of the Fargo storm, Jim told me that it was their loosely secured back door, not the front one, that his mother had tried to protect. But in my mind, I think of Aunt Ted with her arms spread out, resolutely holding the front door as the wind pushed from the other side.

As I waited for the tornado to hit my own house, I wished I could be as fearless as Aunt Ted. I couldn't imagine her meekly agreeing to climb onto a chair, crawl through a window, and stumble across a storm-tossed yard. Lawrence kept wondering aloud if we should go at once, before the storm got worse. "Any minute now!" he warned; a few minutes later, "Are you ready?" But he too waited. The wind blew, the rain pounded, dazzling flashes from the transformer lit up our windows, the darkness of rain returned. Eventually, less than an hour later—an hour measured in long, long minutes—the rain slowed to a rush, then a faint patter. The wind subsided. The windows grew lighter, then transparent. The storm was over.

Nothing awful happened to our house, either. The newspaper next day didn't even call it a tornado, just an unusually strong storm with high straight-line winds. A few shingles were loosened on our roof. Around the corner from us, huge trees were uprooted, as if plucked like giant flowers and strewn across the street. Barricaded by trunks too big to climb over, many streets remained impassible for a week. Although the wind had indeed flung some of the loose transformer wires onto the boulevard a few yards away, none had come near my Volvo. The car was undamaged. So was the boat. Our only real loss was food in our refrigerator and freezer, since electricity was not restored for days. But when I remember that summer storm, I don't think first of spoiled hamburger.

I sometimes wonder if our marriage, which began, for both of us, with love and high expectations, eventually failed because Lawrence thrived on storms, and I didn't. Looking back, I know we had many happy times together, but I often find it depressingly hard to recall them. Instead, quite unfairly, I tend to remember bad weather. That sailboat, for instance. Did we love sailing together on White Bear Lake? No, I had to admit, we didn't. Or at least I didn't.

At first I thought that sailing would be a good way for us to spend time together. Lawrence did not share my enthusiasm for reading, and I did not enjoy tracking the stock market or watching football games. Could we perhaps turn sailing into a common interest? We both were enchanted with our nifty Klepper, and we liked the attention we got if we began assembling it lakeside, piece by piece from its canvas bags. But once we were launched on the water—something that took a frustratingly long time—we ran into trouble.

Before our Klepper, neither of us had ever spent more than a few hours sailing, but we had not lived long in Minnesota, whose license-plate motto was for many years "Land of 10,000 Lakes," before believing that any true Minnesotan owned some kind of boat. With his usual quickness of mind and his graceful, agile body, Lawrence soon taught himself how to handle the Klepper. He was captain, and, not unexpectedly, I was crew. Stationed at the stern, Lawrence handled the rudder and sail, while I tied ropes, shifted my weight as directed, and learned to flatten myself when the boom came around.

Concentrating hard on his task, Lawrence would call out commands. I did my best, but I felt slow and clumsy. When I made a mistake, as I often did, Lawrence shouted at me. No one in my family shouted much, and although Lawrence defended his outbursts as natural Hungarian temperament, I could never get used to them. So I became anxious not to upset him further. The speed at which we were usually moving alarmed me, too. What about the larger boat that was looming on our left—I mean, port—side? Would we be able to stop as we veered toward shore? Could we tack in time?

I gave up on sailing one afternoon after a summer storm. Although the weather forecast predicted possible thundershowers, Lawrence had worked especially hard in his lab that week, with late nights poring over data and mending broken equipment, and he wanted his Saturday on the water. He was sure we'd be able to see any bad weather coming and quickly return to the dock. Though White Bear Lake was large enough to hold a fleet of sailboats quite comfortably, it was just a suburban lake. We would not, he assured me, run into trouble.

But neither one of us had ever experienced an approaching thunderstorm from the middle of a lake. Out on a lake, the sky can feel quite big. A small boat can feel much smaller. At first, looking at faint clouds far in the distance, I was just mildly uneasy. "Should we head in, do you think?" I asked Lawrence timidly. He shook his head. When he was sailing fast, he was utterly absorbed and close to happy. But soon those distant clouds, traveling across the lake like a racing convoy, turned into menacing dark skies directly overhead. What had been a delightful breeze wildly gusted, hard and fast, from unpredictable directions. The storm, we both realized, was moving much faster than we were. Our Klepper began to flap about. Lawrence shouted instructions, I pulled and dipped, the boom whipped back and forth. Lawrence was having increasing difficulty in controlling the boat. Our dock on the far side of the lake now appeared to be impossibly far away.

Just as I was comforting myself with the thought that we were, after all, adequate swimmers, Lawrence seemed to read my mind. "When we go over," he yelled above the sound of waves slapping against the boat, "hold onto the boat if you can! There's nothing we can do about the lightning if it strikes! And forget about your watch! It's as good as gone!" Before setting sail, we usually stashed our few small valuables—car keys, Lawrence's billfold, and my Omega wristwatch, a college graduation gift from my parents—in a storage pocket inside the Klepper. I loved that twenty-one-jewel Omega, the first expensive piece of jewelry I had ever owned. It was not, of course, waterproof. Lawrence did not have to explain that once the boat capsized, even if the watch didn't spill out of the pocket, it would be ruined.

But we didn't capsize. My watch didn't get wet. Somehow, although our boat tipped dangerously several times, Lawrence managed to pilot us back to the dock minutes before the black clouds opened in a deluge. Wet but safe, we hoisted the Klepper out of the water and ran for our car to wait out the storm. As soon as we were inside, Lawrence was genial again. He knew he had done well. He had saved both of us, the boat, his billfold, and my watch. As he almost rubbed his hands with pleasure at our unexpected escape, I realized that he had, astonishingly, actually enjoyed all the excitement. But I was shaking.

Storms haunted our marriage. Who or what was to blame? Whose fault, after all, was the ruined blue rowboat? Another boat, another storm. Another loss. Suppose that wind had never sprung up? Would we have had a happier summer that year, and would that have made a difference? Hadn't the whole unrealistic project been my idea? Although the Klepper, later sold, lasted beyond our struggling marriage, the blue rowboat sank with it.

Or perhaps it didn't. Years later, when James and I drove to Lake Carlos, outside Alexandria, Minnesota, so he could see the lakeshore paradise where my mother had taken my sister and me each summer, we took a leisurely walk down a long dusty road. As we passed a boathouse with sagging door, I stopped abruptly. "Look at that!" I said sharply, tugging at James's sleeve. He looked, puzzled. I was pointing to an old, peeling, half-rotten wooden boat next to the shed. Although it was partly obscured by weeds, it showed patches of faded blue paint clinging to the boards. "Our rowboat! I know that's our rowboat!" I cried. I was surprised to feel so moved.

We owned that rowboat our first summer in Minnesota. In Berkeley, Lawrence and I had discovered that we both liked to fish, and I had promised him that Minnesota would land us in fishing heaven. At Lake Carlos, where my grandfather had bought a long stretch of lakefront, several of my aunts and uncles had built cabins. My mother owned a lot, high above the lake and heavily wooded, but she had never been able to build there. Instead, our little family stayed for a few weeks each August in the old farmhouse where my grandfather had once taken his wife and children for the long, hot summer months.

But Mother told Lawrence and me that since the farmhouse now belonged to another aunt, Mother would be delighted if we could find a way to camp on her lot. She would love to have it used. We could easily do this, I assured Lawrence. We already owned a tent, air mattresses, and a portable stove. Although we would have to lug our gear through thick woods and scratchy brush, we could at least park our car at the nearest relative's cabin. All we needed was an outhouse and a boat.

The outhouse came first. I arranged for a local lumber company to build one—they kept it as a humorous display in their yard for days—and then drag it through the woods to the hole Lawrence had dug. When he was digging, I urged him to make it as deep as possible. "Don't stop yet!" I called over the edge. "More! More!" After many summers at the lake, I knew what happened to outhouse holes that were too shallow.

I still remember our mutual dismay when, finally putting down his spade, he looked up at me and realized he had no way to get out. The hole was deep enough. It was so deep, in fact, that Lawrence, though strong and six feet tall, could not manage to scale the steep walls of hard-packed clay soil. He had dug and dug, without stopping to think what would happen after he had finished digging. I could not help laughing. I was ashamed to realize I felt a secret pleasure to see him trapped down there, fuming in the pit, while I was safely out of reach. But I loyally ran to find Uncle Orie for help—and a ladder.

That left a boat. We needed a rowboat, since we could not afford anything with a motor. With a rowboat, I told Lawrence with the authority of someone who had spent countless August hours dropping a handheld line baited with worms, we could head out to the rock bar just outside Aunt Ted and Uncle Orie's cabin. There we could catch sunnies, rock bass, perch, maybe even walleyed pike. Well, I admitted, I had never actually snagged a walleye, but that didn't mean they weren't out there. When we priced aluminum rowboats, however, we were dismayed to find that they were shockingly expensive. Definitely beyond our budget, Lawrence said gloomily. And we couldn't fish without a boat.

Uncle Orie came once more to the rescue. "Hey, Ted, why don't we let them use Oscar's boat?" he said to his wife. Down in a ravine, where I had swum as a child, an old, thunkingly heavy wooden boat had been beached long ago. It had belonged to my grandfather Oscar, and after his death, no one had bothered to move it. Orie, Lawrence, and I clambered down to the ravine and examined the boat together. Despite its years of neglect, it was in surprisingly good shape. "You'll want to get some good wood and replace some of the rotten pieces there," Orie advised, tapping part of the narrow, curved hull. "But basically, what you need to do is dig out the old putty, recaulk all the seams, and paint it. Then it should be ready to go."

Lawrence wondered how much time and work this would all take, but I convinced him that the two of us, working together, could finish the job in a weekend or two. I was wrong. Very wrong. For much of the summer, Lawrence and I drove for nearly three hours each Friday to Lake Carlos. There we dragged our camping equipment to a space we had cleared on Mother's lot, not far from the new outhouse. Early on Saturday and Sunday mornings, we headed down to the ravine, where, on hands and knees, we scraped, dug, and caulked. I often felt as if a putty knife had become permanently attached to my right hand. Many of those weekend days were hot; on still afternoons, the mosquitoes attacked in droves. We swatted, sweated, and caulked some more.

Neither one of us thought this was fun, but we talked constantly about how much we would enjoy using the refurbished rowboat. As the weekends passed, Lawrence became, quite understandably, more and more fidgety. "The summer will be gone, and we won't have been able to get out on the lake!" he muttered, slapping putty on a newly discovered gap. But finally, toward the end of the summer, on a sunny afternoon, the boat was finished. We had painted it, at my urging, a brilliant blue. I wanted something vivid, cheerful, hopeful.

"I'm taking it out right now," Lawrence announced. He grabbed the two oars we had bought. I am not sure why I did not go with him. Maybe we had quarreled—the atmosphere around the boat had by now become murky with recriminations—and I would have relished the chance to lie in our little tent and read for an hour or two. "I think," I said hesitatingly, "Uncle Orie said we should soak it overnight first. Because it's been dry so long. He said to weight it with stones and leave it in the water close to shore." But Lawrence had waited long enough. He wanted to take the boat out now—not tomorrow, not next week, but *now*. So together we shoved the boat down the ravine and into the water. Seizing the oars, Lawrence rowed out toward the middle of the lake.

But he didn't get very far. It was a calm, clear day, and I could hear him plainly. I couldn't see what was happening at first, but I understood his furious yell: "I'm sinking! Can't you see? I'm sinking!" He began to row frantically toward shore. As he approached, I realized that the boat was indeed very low in the water. When Lawrence finally got close enough so I could wade out to him, I saw that he had taken enough water inside the boat to soak him up to his ankles. Uncle Orie had been right. The old, dry wood needed to absorb enough water to swell and seal all the invisible cracks that our putty hadn't reached.

Lawrence was sputtering with frustration and disappointment. "Hadn't we better put some rocks in it now?" I asked tentatively. "At least the boat is okay. I mean, you could have really been in trouble if you had been farther out. You would have had to swim, and you have all your clothes on. Besides, we could have lost the boat entirely." Lawrence looked up at the sky. It was cloudless. Not a breath of wind stirred the surface of the lake. He must have thought briefly of the labor of dragging the boat back into the shallow water. Then we would have to find enough large stones and carefully heave them, without damaging the planks, into the boat. Yet more work.

"We'll leave it here overnight," he said decisively. "It has plenty of water in it right now. It can soak right where it is." The blue rowboat, glossy and bright with its new paint, lay half in and half out of the lake. In my grandfather's day, someone had cleared a small space on the pebbles to make the ravine a good launching spot for a boat. Our rowboat occupied most of this space. On either side, mostly in the water, were several large boulders. When I was a child, my mother would send me down to this spot with our dirty laundry, so I could scrub it clean on the large rocks. "Leave the boat," Lawrence directed, turning to climb the hill toward our tent. "Let's have dinner."

Although the weather had been clear all day, during the night it changed. Lying in our tent, I could hear the wind begin to ruffle the trees above us. The wind blew harder, and soon rain was pattering on our canvas roof. But I turned over and went back to sleep. This was no frightening thunderstorm, just an ordinary, fast-moving summer rain. No need to worry.

But the next morning, when Lawrence and I took our new poles, spinning reels, and tackle box down to the ravine, ready at last to begin the pleasures of fishing together, we were both shocked into silence. There, blown by wind and tugged by waves farther into the water, lay our rowboat. From yards away, we could see where the hull had been smashed in several places. First the wind had swung the boat against one of the big boulders, and then the waves had banged it back and forth. It was, in a phrase that flashed into my mind from *Moby Dick,* a "stove boat."

I don't remember who spoke first. I would not have been above "I told you so." I have a sharp tongue, and I often found it too easy to use as a weapon. So if I recall our marriage as stormy, Lawrence might well think of its cold biting winds. I do distinctly remember that Lawrence finally turned to me, his face set, and said, "Let's go. Come on, we're packing up. We're going home." And we did.

We never went to Lake Carlos again. For a while, one of my uncles put a padlock on the door and used the outhouse as a toolshed. It stayed there for years, until my mother finally sold the lot, and someone tore it down before building a new cabin. I never knew what happened to the blue rowboat, so carefully salvaged, so earnestly patched up. It was such a bright blue. I like to believe that someone, somehow, managed to restore it again and use it for a while. How else would it have ended up in the weeds by the shambling boathouse down the road? I cannot bear to think of our rowboat as a dead loss.

Our marriage lasted for eleven years. We survived other storms, we enjoyed calmer days, but the weather was unpredictable. We separated and reconciled. We separated yet again. Eventually we began seeing a marriage counselor. Dr. Zamboni, an optimistic man who believed in saving marriages, did his best. What did Lawrence want of me? Would it help if I agreed to watch more television with him in the evenings? But neither Lawrence nor I could hear or understand what the other was trying to say. It was as if a turbulent gale blew away our words in an unforgiving blast. Then, astonishing but thrilling us both, I became pregnant.

For a while I thought, despite knowing better, that our daughter might keep us together. I didn't want a divorce. I loved Lawrence, and I was sure that, in his own way, he loved me as well. Perhaps just as importantly, I could not imagine leaving him. No one in my family had ever been divorced. In the early 1970s, I did not yet have any friends who were divorced. I was terrified at the idea of taking such a drastic step. What would happen to me? Would I be alone the rest of my life?

After a while, Lawrence refused to continue seeing Dr. Zamboni. So I went alone. I wanted support; maybe I just yearned for someone to assure me I wasn't crazy. Listening, comforting, suggesting, Dr. Zamboni finally began to probe, ever so kindly, into my fears. Was it perhaps possible, he inquired, to think about leaving? No, I shook my head, I couldn't. Weren't we married for better or for worse? How could I desert Lawrence?

One afternoon, after I had recounted yet another wounding quarrel, Dr. Zamboni sighed. Perhaps, after so many months, he had heard enough. "Susan," he said with careful patience, "I think you had better face the fact that you are never going to leave this man. You will never, ever leave him. So learn to accept this marriage. Get on with your life." Then our hour was over.

When I went home that night, I could not stop thinking of what Dr. Zamboni had said. It echoed in my mind with a foreboding clarity, like an authoritative forecast of an approaching dangerous storm. Only this one would never end. It would just go on and on. As I lay sleepless in the silent bedroom—Lawrence had been bunking downstairs for many weeks—I had a chilling vision. It wasn't of a storm at all. It was a high, narrow window in a gloomy basement.

Although I hadn't loved all of Henry James's novels, I had read *Portrait of a Lady* several times. Toward the end of the novel, Isabel, James's gallant but unperceptive heroine, realizes that she has made a terrible mistake in marrying Gilbert, an impoverished Italian aristocrat. Gilbert is a man of intelligence and charm, but he is also cold and manipulative. He has long had an affair, Isabel eventually learns, with her supposed friend, Madame Merle. But Isabel believes, with far more persuasive reasons in 1885, culturally and personally, than I had in 1974, that she can never leave her husband.

"She could live it over again, the incredulous terror with which she had taken the measure of her dwelling," James wrote. "Between those four walls she had lived ever since; they were to surround her for the rest of her life. . . . Osmond's beautiful mind gave it neither light nor air; Osmond's beautiful mind indeed seemed to peep down at her from a small high window and mock at her." This, Isabel knows, is the symbolic truth of her life: caught, imprisoned, scorned. Soon afterward, driven by the horror of this realization, she flees for a time to England. Although she decides to return to Italy and Gilbert, partly in order to save her stepdaughter from a forced marriage, James hints—at least to readers who long for hope—that she may not stay imprisoned forever.

That, in my own Midwestern version, was what I also saw of my future. As Dr. Zamboni's firm words rang in my mind, I pictured myself once more in the southwest corner of the basement. I was cowering there, waiting for a storm to carry off the roof over my head. I heard Lawrence's voice, mocking now, urging me to crawl through a broken window and dash through the wind and rain to safety. I remembered how frightened I had been on that storm-riven June afternoon. Looking up at the basement window, I thought I could see Lawrence's face, like the face in James's novel, peering down at me.

The next morning I called Dr. Zamboni. "You said once that if I decided to leave, you could help me find a lawyer," I said. "I need his name. I want to see him right away." Sometime during the night, blown by a wind I had not seen coming, the weather had finally changed.

# Down in the Basement

There are two eyes in the human head—the eye of mystery, and the
eye of harsh truth—the hidden and the open—the woods eye and
the prairie eye. The prairie eye looks for distance, clarity, and light;
the woods eye for closeness, complexity, and darkness.

—Bill Holm, *Prairie Days*

STORMS STILL FRIGHTEN ME. I only enjoy those I watch from
someone else's house. Under another roof, I don't worry about falling
trees, cracked glass, and lethal lightning. For some reason I feel destruction is more likely to strike me when I'm at home. Hiding elsewhere, I
think I have temporarily eluded fate. Shielded by walls and windows not
my own, I listen and watch, as if admiring close-up fireworks.

Frightened or not, I am not sure I would want to live entirely without storms. Since those spectacular outbursts have been part of my
life, the seasons might seem intolerably flat without them. They have
also brought me peculiar gifts. Without the lurking threat of storms, I
might not have known so much about basements. "Go to the southwest corner of the basement, and remain there until you hear the all
clear! Stay tuned to this station for further bulletins!" I always obeyed
that disembodied voice. And without the time I've spent in basements,
my vision of the world might have lacked an indefinable shadowy
dimension.

I don't have a basement anymore. One level of our house is mostly below ground, but James, who designed the house, bridles at calling it anything but "the lower level." It has windows, he argues, with quite a lot of light, and, he adds firmly, I shouldn't lump it into a category with the dark, damp, cellar-like basements we both knew in our childhood. "The orange casserole pot you're looking for is in the basement," I'll tell him. "We don't have a basement," he returns with a bit of a snap. "I assume you mean the lower level?"

But I remember most basements with respect. This respect is particularly attached to storm cellars, the older relatives of basements. A few remained below creaky frame houses as I was growing up in the Midwest. In the movie *The Wizard of Oz,* I breathlessly watched Dorothy, Aunt Em, and Uncle Hiram flee down the steps of their outside storm cellar to escape the oncoming tornado. On the screen, the whirling danger was even more terrifying than in the book—and the storm cellar the only place of refuge. I loved the idea that those hinged doors, folded over the cellar steps, led down to a place of complete security.

The old farmhouse where my mother, sister, and I spent our summer vacations in Minnesota had an outside storm cellar. Steps descended from the kitchen as well, but we almost never went down them. Out of curiosity, I might inch halfway and then stop, peering but uneasy and watchful, on a splintery step before soon retreating. From that black clammy darkness, I could smell an airless odor of mildew, mice droppings, and rank decay. By then I was reading Nancy Drew, Sherlock Holmes, and assorted gory comic books, and I didn't want to discover something unexpected and unnerving in a corner of the cellar.

Just once, I saw the outside cellar doors flung back. My grandfather Oscar, who owned the old house, occasionally drove out to the lake from the nearby town where he lived. My sister and I were a little afraid of Grampa, who was a taciturn, heavy-browed old man, often prickly and given to flashes of outright temper. I wasn't sure Mother liked him that much either, though she reminded us, "He *is* your grandfather, remember, and if it weren't for him, we would not be able to come to Lake Carlos to stay."

That day, probably a Sunday, when Mother would have been cooking a special dinner of baked ham or roast chicken in the cast-iron wood-burning stove that dominated the kitchen, Grampa arrived with a purpose. A woodchuck had gone to ground in the cellar, he said, and he was going to get rid of it. My mother might have seen the animal disappear into a gap in the foundation of the house, or maybe one of my uncles, who had cabins close to us, had somehow noticed it. Then or now, I am not sure why the woodchuck was a threat to him, us, or the house. Did Grampa, who had little to do, and not much excitement in his life, just want to shoot something?

For Grampa had brought a gun. My sister, Karen, and I were fascinated. I'm not sure we had ever seen a shotgun or rifle in the hands of someone we knew, and, except for the volley of rifles at the annual Memorial Day ceremony, we certainly had never watched anyone actually fire one. Nor had we seen a woodchuck. Living in Ames, on a densely settled city block, we were familiar only with birds, squirrels, and the occasional garter snake. So we stood just behind Grampa as he marched to the doors of the storm cellar. He had also brought a flashlight. Shining it into the dark cavernous space, he gave a satisfied grunt.

We looked. There, caught in the light, we could see two gleaming eyes and a dark body. Cowering there in the darkness, it seemed quite small, and very still. Karen, who loved animals, clutched at Grampa. "Don't kill it, Grampa!" she cried. "Don't kill it!" He pushed her away, and my mother, who must have been close by, made Karen and me go indoors. We heard a loud shot, and Karen began to sob wildly. Later I remember staring, with a kind of fascinated horror, at a limp brown shape on the ground outside the cellar doors.

Compared to that cellar, the cement-block basement of our house in Ames was clean and pleasant. Although it had a cement floor, Mother had bought two pieces of printed linoleum to cover part of it. Half the basement was a laundry space, with indoor clotheslines suspended over a sloping drain, and the other half was an area that, in more expensive and newer houses, would eventually become known as a "rec room." Ours was large enough at one end for a wall of shelves and our old-fashioned treadle sewing machine, and at the other for an ironing board, a rocking chair, and a few rough orange crates used as more shelving.

On hot summer days, the basement was the coolest part of the house. Armed with a glass of ice cubes, which I could slowly suck as if they were candy, I would settle into the rocking chair with a book. It was a wonderful place to read on a scorching afternoon. Although a little light filtered through the high narrow windows, the shaded basement felt remarkably remote from the outside world. Except for a little grass and sky, I couldn't see past the deep window wells just outside. My refuge was fairly private, too. Once I'd claimed the one chair, Karen wasn't likely to clatter down the bare wooden stairs, and Mother would only intrude to put another load in the washing machine.

The basement held a deeper refuge. Only part of it was fully dug out. Behind the stairs was a crawl space with a concrete floor. Mother called this, rather formally, "the unexcavated portion." Years later, when I asked Mother about this, she said she hadn't been able to afford a full basement. Although Mother never put on airs with her speech, referring to that orphaned space as "the unexcavated portion" gave it dignity. I thought it was a mysterious sort of place. To enter, I had to pull a chair over to the wall, take off an external screen from the small window that ventilated the space, and then clamber up and over the sill. Once I was inside, I couldn't stand up, remaining hunched—so low that it was nearly impossible for a grown-up—on the icily cold concrete.

Since for much of my adult life I have been a little claustrophobic, disliking windowless rooms and avoiding all possible caves, I am astonished to remember how sometimes I would seek out "the unexcavated portion." (I cannot bring myself to call it anything else.) Perhaps I did this when I was desperate for complete isolation. Once when I was sulking, or furiously angry with my mother or my sister, I fitted the screen back on the window, so no one would know I was inside. I usually took a flashlight (since the space was too dark for any sustained reading), a bed pillow, and a book. I read poetry aloud there; at least once, hurt by something I can't recall, I lay on the pillow and cried with acute self-pity that was satisfyingly amplified in that cold, cramped space.

After a while, even on a blistering July day, I would eventually become chilled. Or the gray concrete all around me, pressing down, would start to feel unnervingly tomblike. Then I would scramble out again, glad to be back in an everyday world of high ceilings and windows whose connection with the sunny day was as near as the swinging outdoor cat flap by my rocking chair. I don't know when I stopped going into the unexcavated portion. But when, in my fifties, I had to clean out the basement of that house, since my mother was moving to a retirement complex, I looked inside the dirty screen to the rough concrete floor and shivered.

That last visit to our basement was unsettling in another way. We did not have an attic, or much other storage space in our one-story house, so the basement became a place that accumulated odd bits of our history. Some of my sister's drawings and paintings, carefully saved since she was a child—my mother knew she would be an artist someday—were stacked on one shelf. On others, in no particular order, Mother had stashed seldom-used vases, a roasting pan, an old hair dryer with an attached hood, a crockery bean pot. Anything that one of us could not quite bear to part with, but never used, often ended up on those crowded shelves.

One whole shelf was a row of empty, dusty Mason jars. Long ago, my mother had stopped preserving and canning. But for years, when I was young, she would labor each summer over the stove, cooking, steaming, sterilizing, until she had filled those jars with burnished tomatoes, peaches, strawberry jam, pickles, beets, and green beans. As winter encroached on our house, we were ready. Our larder was full; our little family would never lack for food. When Mother would send me down the stairs to find a chosen jar, I remember how those rich colors, lined up in a row, glowed in the muffled basement light.

As I was sorting through the shelves, setting some things aside for Goodwill, others for a garage sale, Mother came down the stairs. Her face was set. She was understandably disturbed at how her two grown daughters were whisking through the house, organizing, packing, throwing things away. She had suggested this move, but it was not one she really wanted. "No. I am taking the Mason jars," she said, emphasizing each word, as she pointed to the box where I had heaped them. I protested. Vainly I pointed out that her one-bedroom apartment would barely hold the furniture, books, and records we had already packed. She had no room for empty Mason jars. But Mother was adamant. They would go with her to Northcrest. The basement held memories for my mother too.

I rather miss having a real basement now. No place in our house, much as I love it, offers quite that sense of hidden security, tucked away from storms. Our rooms are airy and light. Except for our laundry and furnace room, every living space has at least one window. So when severe storms begin to move through the Twin Cities, and weather forecasters, spotting ominous funnel clouds, warn their audiences to flee to a sheltered spot, I don't usually bother. Our basement—I mean, the lower level—doesn't feel any safer than the rest of the house, which, James assures me, is certainly not going to be in the direct path of a tornado. I do my best to believe him.

# A Window on the Weather

Spring and Summer, Fall and Winter and Spring
After each other drifting, past my window drifting!
       . . . looking out the window by day
My thought ran back, it seemed, through infinite time . . .
       —Edgar Lee Masters, "Rebecca Wasson," *Spoon River Anthology*

ONE CHEERLESS MARCH MORNING, I turned the newspaper page and stopped at a somber photograph. A middle-aged, grizzled man was stooping over a fallen cow, staring down at the dying animal with tight-lipped helplessness. Behind him I could see miles of empty Nebraska plains, shrouded with snow. The man had a jacket on, but he looked cold. Above the accompanying story, the headline read: "Poverty on the Farm."

It was a sobering piece. After putting the paper down, I went to my kitchen window. Outside in our compact, neatly fenced yard, the rainbow-colored windsock was twisting gently. We too had wind. As I drove to the grocery store, I was thinking about the picture. How protected I was, how safely removed from that biting prairie wind. Living in the city, I could reach my garage in moments. And if I really didn't like what I saw outside, now that I was retired from teaching, I might not have to leave the house at all.

Like most urbanites, I have seen much of my weather from behind a window. Midwesterners are deeply attached to their windows. When my widowed mother decided in 1949 to build a tightly budgeted house, she was proud that she could afford a "picture window," something fairly new in Ames. This expanse of sheet glass proclaimed modernity and luxury, much as multipaned glass windows in Tudor England indicated an owner's status and wealth.

At Hardwick Hall in Derbyshire, England, a mansion built in the late sixteenth century, Bess of Hardwick, a flamboyant widow, commanded her architect to adorn her magnificent house with a dazzling array of windows. The house reflects her personality. Ames had its own small-scale Bess of Hardwick. Once in the early 1950s, as we walked past a large new rambler in our neighborhood, a girlfriend confided to me that a woman who had recently divorced her husband—then an event also stunningly new in Ames—had built it all for herself. My friend's mother had heard it had cost the extraordinary sum of $27,000. "And look," my friend urged, "it has *two* picture windows." And it did. I was almost as impressed by the double picture windows as by the divorce.

What did most picture windows look out on? In most cases, not much. Through her plate glass, the divorcee would have seen only a street lined with young trees and modest ramblers whose (single) picture windows stared back at her. Our own picture window opened onto an uneven brick patio, a bit of garden and grass, and the blank side of a neighbor's garage.

But when we wanted to know what the weather was like, we depended on the picture window to tell us. Looking through it, we could see the last smears of dirty white snow finally disintegrate in the warm spring sunshine. We watched, riveted, as a summer thunderstorm flattened grass and beat down flowers in the garden. In autumn, glancing through the window, we noticed how frosty winds were whipping fallen leaves around the yard. On silent winter afternoons, we could hear the whoosh and swish of thick snow as it swept over the picture window like a flowing white drape.

For most Midwesterners, picture windows serve as giant screens for an ongoing production, which we call, with self-conscious pretension, our "theater of the seasons." This image of weather as entertaining theater might not often occur to a farmer who, in the midst of a blinding snowstorm, had to grope his way to a barn to feed or milk his stock or to a snowplow operator trying to pilot his lumbering machine down a rural road. Suggesting a proscenium arch, with an onstage drama safely separated from us, the phrase defines us as urban onlookers.

Our view is often skewed. Watching the weather behind a window, I see it only in squares and patches. When wind and thundery rain beat against the glass, I am drawn to my window, wishing I could see more of the storm, where it is coming from, what it is doing out there. I know I am glimpsing only a framed snapshot.

That is one reason I have hung a large print of Magritte's *Euclidean Promenades* on our wall. In this oil painting from 1955, an easel stands in front of a large window. Framed by heavy dark drapes, the closed window looks out on a serene stylized landscape. Two fairy-tale towers rise among trees, with distant tall buildings, looking like urban chateaus, against a robin's-egg-blue sky.

The unattended easel is provocative. Placed on it is a transparent square—a see-through canvas, in a way—nearly as large as the lower pane of the window. So the viewer, already strictly positioned inside a room, finds herself looking first through the glass, as if it were a lens, and only then at the scene outside. She sees everything through the window at a double remove. Every time I look at this painting, I wonder how that square of transparency, which seems so disarmingly clear, might yet be refracting my vision. Does it distort? Does it merely frame? Is framing itself a distortion? Is my view of the world often unconsciously filtered through a glass?

I think of that Nebraska farmer, the aging grizzled man—*weathered* is of course the proper adjective—bending over his fallen cow. Yes, he may have a heated pickup. Maybe he can return to a heated farmhouse. But he works outdoors, and good or bad weather will unambiguously affect his crops, stock, and income. He may no longer live in a sod hut or drag a plowshare over unbroken prairie, but he has to confront the weather directly. Urban Midwesterners may focus so intensely on the weather because we too want to maintain a connection to the natural world.

I often feel I have lost that connection. Mostly these days I see the sky out of my window. Even on my city walks, the sky is hedged in by buildings. Since Midwesterners grow up with lots of sky, we become addicted to it. Those of us in cities know that not far beyond our suburbs—just beyond Minneapolis, Omaha, Fargo, Indianapolis, Des Moines, Sioux Falls, Cincinnati, Detroit, or Chicago—the land stretches for miles and miles under an enormous sky. It is quiet out there, roomy, peaceful. Beyond our noisy, hectic lives lies something else. I carry that sense of sky like a promise.

Once or twice a year, when James and I have driven from Minneapolis to Ames, we take the long way home and turn off the freeway onto county roads. Oh, how we widen our eyes as the landscape unrolls before us. Grain elevators, country churches, farmhouses, barns and silos, brown muddy rivers, leftover bits of woods, neat rows of windbreaks, and clusters of small towns are only brief punctuation marks under an endless sweep of sky.

On those back roads, we also come face to face with the weather. Nothing impedes weather on the prairies. We can see it sweeping toward us from miles away—dark roiling clouds, floating white mountains, streaky rainsqualls. When it snows on the back roads, it snows everywhere, and we drive through an endless tunnel of whirling flakes. When it rains, we are in the midst of Noah's flood. On a very hot summer day, the heat is in fact quite visible, a shimmer rising from the concrete ahead. And we are right there, in the midst of everything. If a tornado were to roll out of a black cloud, we might not be able to outrun it, but at least we would see it coming. When we finally arrive back at our city house on its narrow shady lot, I think we both feel rather dazed but contented, as if all that sky has somehow washed our minds clean.

I remember how, many years ago, a window on the sky brought me that same sense of contentment. I now think of those nights as partly a weather story, a search for calm after storm. When her father and I separated, Jenny was only two, and although she saw her father frequently, in the early years he seldom kept her overnight. So when he did, it was a treasured gift of a quiet house, undisturbed hours, all to myself. Most weeks I scurried and rushed: teaching classes, meeting with students, caring for my daughter, cooking and cleaning, running errands. As I attended committee meetings, called doctors, talked with friends, and occasionally entertained, I was surrounded by voices. But when Lawrence left with Jenny for an overnight, I was suddenly off-duty. Not needed. Not required to be present.

As the door closed behind them, I felt a quiver of utter relaxation. What selfish time lay ahead! If I had to spend a few hours grading papers, answering mail, or doing laundry, I made sure I stopped by five or six o'clock. Encircled by companionable silence, I ate a pickup supper. Then, moving with deliberate slowness, I would put on a nightgown, pull up the shades, and climb into bed. There I lay, not expecting to sleep, not even wanting to sleep. I just lay in bed, comfortable, entirely peaceful, and looked out the window at the sky.

In the house Jenny and I shared until I married James, my bedroom had two sets of windows. One narrow one, at the left of my bed, stared too closely at the neighbors' side windows. So I left a filmy curtain drawn over that window until it got dark. The two double windows at the foot of my bed opened onto my backyard and alley. I kept those curtains open. Although I couldn't see a great deal of sky, I saw enough.

As I lay on my bed for hours, watching darkness steal into the room, I let my thoughts wander uninterrupted: the days ahead, places I had traveled, people I had known. But mostly, drowsy but still awake, I looked out the windows at the weather. All weather on those nights was magical. When snow fell, it caught the light from my neighbors' house and the streetlights in the alley, so I could watch it descend in silent sparkles. Although I don't sleep well in heat, I relished the warm summer breezes drifting lazily through my open window. Tossing off my sheet, I wiggled my toes, as if I were lying on a beach, sinking into the sand. I especially loved a gentle rain. Listening to its tapping on the panes, I felt myself drift into the sky.

Happily married now to James for so many years, I no longer look forward to nights by myself. When we have to be apart, I sleep uneasily, knowing he is not in arm's reach. But I remember with pleasure those long-ago hushed evenings, when I lay alone in bed, half awake and half asleep, watching the dusk turn into dark. In those slow-moving hours, I found something I needed. The weather, my Midwest weather, grounded me, settled me down, and reminded me who I was.

My windows offered safety and security then. Now I know better. Even city dwellers discover the unpredictability and frightening power of Midwest weather. High winds blow down city trees (and occasionally smash picture windows). Tornadoes wipe out whole neighborhoods. Heat turns city apartments deadly, especially for the elderly and infirm. Ice and snow transform freeways into terrifying skating rinks. When the power goes out, or rain forces its way into ceilings and basements, or roads become blocked with drifting snow, we can feel, however briefly, that we are closer to the pioneers than we like to think.

Every winter I read in the newspaper about someone who, stranded in a snowstorm, tried to seek shelter and died of exposure before finding it. I used to assume, a little smugly, that this was unlikely for someone who had a house in town. Then, many years ago, I was shaken out of such certainty. Jenny was six or seven then. Every morning, quite early, she had to catch a school bus. As soon as she was out the door, walking one block to the street corner where she would be picked up, I would gather my books, papers, and lunch and hurry to the garage. I was anxious to arrive at my office so I could have a little time to prepare for my morning classes. Some mornings Jenny dawdled, and I scolded and fussed. If she missed her bus—and she sometimes did—I had no choice but to drive her to school myself and arrive late, apologizing, at my own class.

Although I adored my only child, and I was a highly protective mother, I was also a frequently harassed, impatient single parent. So one bitterly cold winter morning I snapped with unusual fierceness at Jenny about her tardiness. "I'm sick and tired of having to take you to school," I think I said. Or maybe I felt meaner: "Don't think I'm going to take you to school again! If you miss the bus, you can just stay home." I can still hear how angry my tone must have been. I helped her zip up her bright-red snowsuit—it was well below zero that morning—before she slammed the door and rushed toward the corner.

Usually I backed out of our garage, turned at the other corner, and zoomed toward the college without looking back. But that morning, for some reason, I turned in the opposite direction, making a slight detour so I could drive past Jenny's bus stop. Because she hadn't come back, head sulkily down, shuffling her clunky snowboots, I assumed she'd safely caught her bus and was now at school.

Snow had fallen so heavily that winter that huge ice-hardened mounds blocked many of the sidewalk intersections. Looking from our front door, I couldn't see much of the bus corner except heaped snow. But as I passed, I braked in shock. There, huddled like a small red elf—a crouching, dispirited elf who had lost all her magic power—was my daughter. Enveloped by the mountainous snow, she was close to invisible. Except for her red snowsuit, I might have missed her. Certainly no neighbors would ever have seen her. Nor could she have gone home if she'd wanted to. Since she was too young to be alone, she had no key.

I didn't want to think about how much longer Jenny might have waited. Or what would have happened to her in that glittering cold. Scooping her up, I whisked her into the car. Filled with self-recrimination—How could I have been so bad-tempered? Scared her so that she didn't dare come home?—I then hurried her to my office. She could warm up there until after my class. Even before we arrived, Jenny had stopped shivering. By the time she was soothed, petted, and settled in my big desk chair, she was almost pleased to have missed her bus. But I was trembling a little when I walked into my classroom.

I think about that cold winter morning sometimes. The memory makes me tremble. In an echo of the familiar rote warning of Midwest broadcasters, it reminds me how dangerous it is to take the weather for granted. But I am also haunted by that image of a little girl, growing colder and colder, her red snowsuit bright against the white snow, for other, more complicated reasons. It strums a string of guilt that vibrates too easily in mothers like me, mothers who know they made some serious mistakes. I got it very wrong that morning. But it also reminds me of how vulnerable we all are. Jenny. Me. All of us. We do not stay safely behind windows. Out there, the weather is always waiting.

We were lucky that morning. Many of us who live in Midwest towns and cities trade weather stories, mostly, thank heavens, about lucky escapes. I have my favorites: sitting nervously in the passenger seat, for instance, as Jenny, then in her midtwenties, drove along a Minneapolis freeway in a torrential summer rain. We could not see anything but the faint taillights of a car just ahead of us. Passing semis constantly drenched that spark of light. Finally, when we pulled to the side of the road, hoping that no one would rear-end our car in the blinding storm, Jenny said cheerfully, "Don't worry. Remember when James and I drove home in the flood?"

I remembered. Another rainstorm, unpredicted and fierce. Record inches of rain—four? six? eight?—fell in an hour. Driving home together from our Wisconsin retreat, Jenny and James found themselves dodging geysers of water that erupted from storm sewers. Rivers ran in the streets. Cars stalled everywhere. At our house, I listened anxiously to the television. Reporters were eagerly gathering anecdotes of catastrophe and rescue. I knew the two people I loved most in the world were somewhere out there, on the road, in the midst of it all.

When they did arrive safely, Jenny was bubbly with excitement. "I thought it was neat," she said. "James just kept going. We plowed through the water like a boat. We had to veer into side streets, because so many cars were stuck on the main drag. He said we couldn't stop or we'd never get started again. You wouldn't believe how high the water was! It washed over the hood. But we rocked along, no matter what. It was a little scary, but I felt sort of like a pioneer." There it was again: weather trying to sweep us all back to the open prairie. Away from windows.

I remember another rainstorm when my sheltered city life was no longer safe from weather. I think of this particular rainy morning as a balance, or a counterweight, to the snowy morning at the bus stop, because this too is a rescue story. Only this time, Jenny rescued me. Or was it one of Nancy's angels? Nancy, a loving friend who died of cancer a few years ago, was deeply grounded in the kind of spirituality most of us can only envy. She firmly believed in the underlying goodness of the world, the constant presence of grace, the possibility of angels. Since she lived near me, we often walked together around Lake Harriet and argued animatedly about my more jaundiced views of life.

On that warm, humid morning, I was cross when I left the house to meet Nancy. Jenny was home for a vacation—I think she was in college then, nineteen or twenty—and she was, as usual, sleeping late. I can't now remember exactly why I was so cross, but I think I'd asked her to do something, maybe take out the garbage or clean up her dirty dishes, and she hadn't done it. We often quarreled in those years, not constantly or always dramatically, but we were now two adult women trying to find ways to live independently with each other.

A storm was clearly brewing that morning. Hot, heavy weather had descended on Minneapolis a few days before, and the newspaper predicted rain in the afternoon, maybe tonight. Clouds had already begun to pile up in the west, thick and dark, but since it was early, about eight o'clock, I thought Nancy and I could walk around the lake before the storm hit. We conferred briefly on the phone and agreed to take our umbrellas, just in case.

For the first fifteen or twenty minutes of our circular walk, which usually lasted close to an hour, I complained to Nancy about Jenny. My daughter was spoiled, I said, and selfish. She thought only of herself. She was driving me crazy, and just this morning she had said this, or done that, or refused to do this or that. I was not in a forgiving mood. After listening sympathetically, and laughing at little at my vehemence, Nancy spoke up gently in Jenny's defense. Had I considered . . .? Might Jenny be . . .? Should I try . . .? A year or so before, Nancy had announced she wanted to become Jenny's honorary godmother, and she took her self-appointed responsibility seriously. Hmmph, I grumbled. What did Nancy know?

Meanwhile the clouds had become darker and more threatening. We were halfway around the lake, on a three-mile path, when the storm broke over our heads. At first we merely grimaced and put up our umbrellas. But quickly it became clear that this was no ordinary, quick-soaking rain. Thunder boomed continually as if the sky were an iron sheet someone was obsessively pounding with a stone mallet, a sheet that was cracking and splitting under the strain. But it was the lightning that frightened us. Bolts of blue-white light tore through the clouds and darted toward the lake, so much lightning that it seemed a circuit breaker had shorted out somewhere in those menacing dark clouds. Smash, crack. Almost no pause. Then smash, crack. Smash, crack.

Nancy and I looked at each other. We were now halfway around the lake. Her house was as far as mine, at least a half-hour walk, even at a fast pace. Tall trees, obvious lightning catchers, lined our path and the street a few yards away. The broad expanse of Lake Harriet beckoned the lightning, offering an alluring target, tempting it to strike. And our umbrellas! "Susan, you realize that these metal umbrellas are perfect conductors?" asked Nancy uneasily. The rain poured down, streaming off the umbrellas as if we'd been standing under a torrential waterfall. Already our legs were soaked with splashes from the water as it hit the pavement at our feet. With the sudden rain, the temperature had also dropped precipitously, and we were both beginning to feel chilled.

Just then, as Nancy and I, though capable and efficient women, were standing in helpless indecision about what to do next, I heard a car horn. We both turned toward the street. There, pulled over to the curb, windshield wipers beating valiantly against overwhelming odds, was my old reliable Honda. And there, gesturing urgently from the window she'd rolled down, oblivious to the rain soaking her face, was my daughter. "Get in!" she yelled. Still a little in shock—who would drive in a storm like this?—we paused for the briefest of moments. Then we both furled our umbrellas and dashed for the car.

Once I was inside, I turned incredulously to Jenny. My daughter, whose fast driving often irritated me, was maneuvering slowly, carefully, with great competence, through the rain. "But how did you know?" I asked. "You were asleep when I left. I know, because I looked in on you. You were buried under the blanket as if you were going to sleep all day."

Jenny grinned. She was, understandably, proud of her rescue. "Well, the storm woke me up. And when I got upstairs, I saw you weren't there. I remembered you had mentioned you were going to walk with Nancy this morning. I could tell the storm was getting worse, and I knew you were out there, somewhere around the lake. I got scared. So I figured I had better come and get you."

Nancy looked at me. Then she said to Jenny, firmly and with great pleasure, "Jenny, you are really wonderful. I don't know what would have happened without you. It is a miracle you woke up and figured out where your mother was. As far as I'm concerned, this morning, you were an angel from heaven. Right, Susan?" I looked with unbelieving gratitude at my daughter. I nodded. "Absolutely," I said. Jenny beamed. And, years later, on days when I'm angry with her—and there are still a few of those days—I sometimes think of that rain-soaked morning on the Lake Harriet path.

Jenny is long grown and gone now, living in a distant city, and although we keep in close touch, I realize that most of my parenting is done. I dispense advice, often unasked, and I worry, but I know that I am no longer responsible for her welfare. Yet my mothering instinct remains deeply embedded. I do not think it will ever really disappear. After so many years of listening for warning sounds in the night, from a croupy cough to late footsteps on the stairs, I will hear a baby start to cry—in a restaurant, a strange house, or an airport lounge—and I turn, with automatic anxiety, to see if it is mine.

A year or two after Jenny graduated from college, when I was quite happily adjusted to the pleasures of an empty nest, yet another rainstorm jolted me into a reminder of what it had really meant for me to be a mother. Weather, ever changing, never entirely predictable, is a rich metaphor for parenting. At the most basic level, parents try to protect their children from all the hazards, including weather, that assault the young and vulnerable. We zip their snowsuits, button their coats, make them wear their boots. Don't get frostbite, we tell them, and don't go near the thin ice on the lake. Come right home after school. Come in, come in, it is cold outside. One of Bob Dylan's classic hits, though it masquerades as a love song, seems to me the wistful wail of a little boy who wanted his mother: "'Come in,' she said, 'I'll give you shelter from the storm.'"

Another hot summer day and night, another rainstorm. Another time I was impelled to step beyond my window. But this time I was alone at our blufftop retreat high above the Mississippi River in Wisconsin. James was too busy to stay past the weekend, and I had decided to remain by myself for a few days. Although other weekend houses line the bluffs nearby, each is hidden on many wooded acres, and most stand empty during the week. So when I turn out the lights at night, I am surrounded by silence and unbroken darkness.

That evening I ate supper out on our deck and watched the robin on her nest. The deck is cantilevered over the bluff, and James designed it with great care so that it would not displace any of the tall old trees on our slope. One gnarled branch of an ancient oak had now actually grown over a corner of the deck, so close that it dipped and swayed in heavy winds just inches away. Winds often blow hard and fierce across the wide river, which is why we named the house Wind Whistle.

The robin clearly didn't know about the wind when she built her nest. We had had robins' nests before, mainly slung over our front light or wedged securely into the beams of our garage. But this robin had decided to raise her family in a slight crook at the tip of the old oak branch. The small V-shaped crook offered just enough room for a nest, but the branch wavered with the slightest breeze. When James and I saw the nest, we both shook our heads. But so far the robin had done well. Just a few days ago, the eggs had hatched, and now she hovered protectively over three new nestlings. They were so small her body could cover them completely.

On that July evening, I went to bed quite early. Since the night was utterly still, hot and humid, my windows were wide open. It was, I knew, just the kind of night for a thunderstorm. That didn't worry me. James had so skillfully designed the sturdy house, and the carpenters had built it so well, that it did not quiver in the strongest wind. I might lose electricity for some hours, or even days, but I would be safe and snug. I did not think about the robin.

But when I woke, sometime past midnight, I thought of her immediately. Lightning was flashing like constantly blinking lights through the trees, and gusts of rain were just beginning to batter the window glass. I got up to close the windows, and then I crawled back into bed and tried to go back to sleep. But I couldn't. The storm was growing louder and more tumultuous, so that the wind was now howling and moaning around the house. Worse, I couldn't forget the robin on her nest. The rain fell harder and faster. The wind blew louder. What was happening to the robin? How could she possibly stay on the nest in such a wind? What had become of those baby birds?

Finally I could no longer stand it. I got out of bed again, hastily pulled on a rain jacket over my nightgown, walked through the dark house, and stepped out onto the deck. Rain blew steadily into my face, and a blast of wind pushed me back against the sliding door. But there, as I soon saw in a lightning glare, was the robin. She was sitting on her nest, her glistening wet wings spread over it, her nestlings—I hoped—safe beneath. The branch swung as if someone were violently shaking it, back and forth, the old wood creaking with the strain. Impossible, I thought, that the nest can stay in its wobbly perch much longer. At any moment, it would crash to the ground. But the mother robin had no intention of leaving. Clinging to the rocking nest, she absorbed the force of the storm, protecting the baby birds with her life.

I stood there for a few minutes, getting soaked by the rain, watching the nest jerk and swing. I felt both sadness and a kind of awe. Of course I realized that I was being foolish; birds are not humans. But mothers are mothers. If I had to, I think I too would have stretched out my wings and shielded my child in just that way. I turned and went back inside, protected behind my window. Once again in bed, I kept picturing the robin until I finally fell into an uneasy sleep. The rain seemed a little less, the wind a bit quieter. But in the morning I was sure I would find the scrawny nestlings in a broken heap, lying on the ground near the ruined nest.

The morning was clear, calm, and sunny. The humidity had blown away with the storm, and only a light breeze flapped a little at my blinds. I dreaded stepping out on the deck. But there, astonishingly, was the robin. She sat quietly now on the nest, which barely moved in the breeze. Later, when she flew off to find worms, I counted: three nestlings, safe inside. I did not know how she had done it, but she had. When James called me during breakfast, I excitedly told him my story. "She's still there!" I almost shouted. "She rode out the storm!" "Of course she did," he said. He was not surprised. But then he has six grown children of his own.

I have never forgotten that robin. She taught me something about doing what you have to do, no matter what is happening out there, no matter what the weather. And of course she reminded me that, much as I like to think I live securely behind my windows, as long as I care about anyone, I don't. I cannot keep those I love, let alone myself, separated from the world and its dangers. They must step out into the storm, and so must I. We have to leave our windows and hope for the best. In the end, we are all at the mercy of the weather.

# Weather Words

So brilliant was the snow-glare that when she entered the house she
saw the door-knobs, the newspaper on the table, every white surface as
dazzling mauve, and her head was dizzy in the pyrotechnic dimness. . . .
The world was so luminous that she sat down at her rickety little desk
in the living-room to make a poem. (She got no farther than "The sky
is bright, the sun is warm, there ne'er will be another storm.")
—Sinclair Lewis, *Main Street*

Several years ago, when our doctor told me gently but firmly
that I had high blood pressure, I panicked. It was not just that I felt
damaged, old, and fearfully mortal. But, as he went on to explain that
he would now prescribe a little of this and some of that, and eventually we would control this problem, I had almost stopped listening. I
had fastened on the words, "high pressure." I had heard those words
of warning all my life.

High pressure: that was how I learned to describe the academic
institutions I chose, my often tense life as a scholarship student, years
of graduate school, looming deadlines for my dissertation, finally
a precarious tenure-track job, and at last the jammed schedule of a
working single mother. When I occasionally complained of fatigue,
anxiety, and migraines, my sympathetic friends tried to reassure me,
"Well, of course! You're under awfully high pressure."

But I also understood high pressure as something else, something mysterious and uncontrollable. High pressure was not only a

psychological state, it was also an inescapable aspect of ever-changing, unpredictable weather. How could I alter the very air in which I drew each breath? Who could do anything about the weather?

Living most of my life in the Midwest, I grew up hearing about the weather. Even if I didn't pay attention, someone was talking about it. Weather words blared out of the car radio, the television, the front page of the newspaper. Some of them, clear and simple, I understood immediately: "storm warning," for example, and "heat wave." Nobody needed to explain to me what "showers" meant, or "tornado watch" or "snow flurries." But "high pressure" and "low pressure," terms weather forecasters used frequently, remained murky.

From time to time, after I had studied just enough minimal science to fulfill my high school and college requirements, I would temporarily grasp the basic principles of air pressure. Then I would promptly forget them. Not long ago, I acquired a copy of *Prairie Skies,* written in 1990 by veteran weather forecaster and meteorologist Paul Douglas. Currently a newspaper columnist and popular television weatherman in the Twin Cities, Mr. Douglas loves weather, weather of all kinds, and especially Midwest weather. (His first chapter is titled "Welcome to the Super Bowl of Weather.") He also writes with authoritative intelligence lightened by humor, so, eager to smarten up, I checked his index for "barometric pressure."

Here is what Paul Douglas told me on page fifty-eight: "Although it's hard to imagine, the air overhead is a fluid, with waves, troughs, and crests much like the sea. The atmosphere exerts a downward pressure or weight, capable of displacing a column of mercury to a height of about thirty inches. A drop in air pressure usually implies deteriorating weather, a rising barometer hinting at a clearing trend." (I noted "usually implies" and "hinting at." Not much certainty here, which didn't surprise me. That's weather for you.)

Yes, I silently agreed, air pressure *is* hard to imagine. I don't do well with "displacing a column of mercury," which is something I've never done. Instead, since I have a hopelessly literal mind, I picture a sort of invisible box in the sky, filled with something colorless and viscous, like a thin sugar syrup. An invisible weight, resembling the plunger in a hand-press French coffeemaker, pushes down on the syrupy air. The air gets squashed. It is now under uncomfortably high pressure. Then the plunger lifts back up. Whew, the air lets out a sigh, glad to be free again. Plenty of space, relax, let go. Thus, low pressure.

These are not, however, quite the conclusions Paul Douglas, or any other meteorologist, has in mind, since, meteorologically speaking, I gather that high pressure is usually good (clearing skies) and low pressure maybe not so good (deteriorating). I wish I could remember those equivalents, but I won't. I acquired a baffled distrust of barometers years ago. When my widowed mother remarried, Buell, my new stepfather, installed an expensive barometer on our living room shelf. It was a fine-looking scientific instrument, with tubes, several dials, and a polished hardwood case. With a little guidance from Buell, who was eager to help, I tried to read and interpret it. I never succeeded. I could not mark properly whether the levels were rising or falling. Nor could I correlate what was happening inside the barometer with what was going on outside.

"Storm's coming," Buell would say. "The barometer's falling." (Or was it rising?) But the storm didn't necessarily come. "Better weather tomorrow. The barometer's rising." (Or was it falling?) Tomorrow seemed much the same, or worse. Sometimes he would become quite excited. A dramatic drop, or rise, in his barometer, coupled with a specific kind of sky, could mean a blizzard, or a tornado, or another event that might imperil his new home and family, about which he cared intensely. My mother would half-listen, murmuring appreciative or concerned agreement ("Yes, we may need to go to the basement later," or "Do keep an eye on the sky, then, dear"). But she would smile a little at me. She didn't really believe in the barometer either.

Still, I heard a lot about high pressure and low pressure. They were words that indicated change, possible trouble, even catastrophe. They became part of my background vocabulary; no wonder I heard my doctor's diagnosis with subliminal alarm. Pressure, in turn, became linked to another weather word, "front," one more brush stroke to my view of the world. "Fronts" sound ominous. Every day, on the back page of my newspaper, I can see on a weather map the actual wavy lines of one or more, an immense front of something moving across our part of the country, pushed or shoved one way or another by an equally immense front of something else. I grew up thinking of fronts either as sharp, knifelike wedges, slicing through the sky, or, if the weather looked stormy, as piled-up clouds rolling across the plains like monstrous tidal waves.

We exist in the Midwest, I came to believe, totally at the mercy of fronts. Traveling immense distances, whooshing over the Rockies, scorching across the Great Plains or screaming down from the Arctic tundra, they rush irresistibly over us, one front after another. Our true boundaries are not the state lines of Iowa, or Nebraska, or North Dakota. No, we get our weather from far, far away, not just from off-shore breezes in Virginia or a little squall moving up from the Caro-linas. My friends on the East Coast (who never come to visit) speak, patronizingly, of where I live as "flyover land." Little do they know. What about our fronts? We live, quite literally, on the cutting edge.

Over my lifetime, weather forecasters, armed with increasingly elaborate and sensitive equipment, have become much more capable of predicting impending disaster. And they are eager to tell us about it. So more and more, those of us living in the Midwest hear, over radio and television, the clanging toll of two weather words: "watch" and "warning." They differ in volume, but they both sound an alert, like an omniscient mother calling loudly as her children straggle out the door: "Watch out! Be careful! Now, this is my last warning!" On FM radio, a brisk voice, with barely subdued enthusiasm, breaks into a lilt-ing Mozart quartet: "We interrupt this program to bring you the fol-lowing bulletin from the National Weather Service . . ." On television, while a sitcom rattles on, unsubdued by the terrors of life, a banner begins to run across the bottom of the screen. It reads, with excruci-ating slowness, like a Times Square news flash: "A storm warning has been issued for the following counties. . . . This warning is in effect until 10:00 P.M." Watch. Wait. Hope you can survive until 10:00 P.M.

A watch, says Paul Douglas, is issued "when conditions are ripe" for a severe storm. A storm warning goes one step further, taking us to the brink of catastrophe, "when there is a high probability that a storm will actually strike." In winter, we watch for severe snow-storms and blizzards; in spring and summer, thunderstorms and tornadoes. In fall, we get whatever is left over. During a single year, Midwesterners are warned a lot. We watch a lot. We wait.

During tornado season, we can escalate further. If a tornado has actually been sighted, an emergency siren begins to sound in the Twin Cities, and, for all I know, in other towns and cities as well. It is a bloodcurdling shriek that fades and swells, often muffled by high winds, then unexpectedly blasts through the trees. I am not sure where our particular siren lives—probably a local fire station—but it seems to be peculiarly disembodied, howling, in faint despair, from an unknown cave.

When I hear that dire moan, I want to know what the siren has seen that I haven't. It is impossible not to want to glance out the window. Paul Douglas warns about this: "At all costs, avoid looking out the windows! Your first reaction to a tornado warning may be to run to the nearest window for a closer look, but you're asking for trouble. Shredded plate-glass windows hitting human flesh at upwards of two hundred miles per hour can have some very unpleasant effects."

I repeat Paul's wisdom to James as I tug him toward the lower level of our house. But James is immune to weather words. They do not exercise their totemic magic on him. So he pleasantly but firmly resists; he has no intention of missing the fun. Out he goes, peering at the sky from our front porch, or climbing to our rooftop deck, above the trees, so he can see what is happening. Once, when I told him about the summer storm, so many years before, when my first husband and I had huddled in our basement, waiting for the house to collapse on top of us, he grinned. "Oh, yes, I remember that storm. Do you know what I was doing? A friend of mine and I went up to the roof deck to see the trees as they fell down. Our wives kept calling to us to come inside, but we were having a wonderful time."

So the constant stream of weather words that flows around us doesn't affect everyone. But because I pay such close attention to words, they have certainly affected me. I would have been a worrier anyway. My mother worried, my sister worries (though in different ways), and I grew up with a personality prone to watching, waiting, and expecting the worst. The more I learned about weather, the more I found to worry me.

Consider, for example, the phrase "black ice." On certain cold winter days, when the temperature sinks well below zero, a film of ice can form on deceptively dry highways. Weather bulletins will warn drivers to slow down, be careful, take no chances. This is how Paul Douglas explains it: "At higher temperatures, hydrocarbon emissions and water evaporate after leaving your vehicle's tail pipe. But when the mercury slips into negative numbers, that water freezes directly onto roadway surfaces (a process known as deposition)."

I hear a report of black ice with a shiver. A nervous driver anyway, I am wary of snow-packed streets. But at least I can see the snow. Black ice is an almost invisible sheen. It seems unconscionably malevolent, an evil trickster hiding on an innocuous stretch of road, waiting to snatch an unsuspecting car (probably mine) and whisk it into a spin, a ditch, a crash. "Black ice" has something of the resonance for me that Melville found in the whiteness of the whale: more than mere color or absence of color. Something else entirely.

Of course I am not frightened by all weather words. I am, in fact, fond of some of them. "Snow flurries," for instance: a lovely, light-hearted phrase. From October until May, Minnesotans hear quite a bit about snow flurries. They are not threatening; they elicit neither watch nor warning. Flurries are only brief, wispy gusts of snow, enough for a "dusting" (another often-used weather word here) but not "measurable" (and thus serious). A snow flurry looks like a white lace fishnet being shaken lightly in front of our window. Once outside, I can feel it brush against my cheek or land briefly on my woolly hat before whirling off again. A flurry in October is a chilly whisper foretelling winter; an April flurry is winter's last, reluctant, prolonged farewell.

Midwesterners who can stay quietly at home, electricity and heat intact, may be pleased and excited by the word "blizzard." (Dairy Queen has invented a gooey ice-milk treat, packed with chunky sweets, called a Blizzard.) Blizzards, as most people know, are infrequent, highly dramatic, blinding snowstorms, the kind of storm that transforms a city into soft white sculpture. (Yes, they also disrupt city services, make travel hazardous, and isolate the vulnerable.)

My other favorite weather words are phrases that invoke flashes of personal history. "Well, these are the dog days of summer," I remember hearing my mother say resignedly, usually sometime in the middle of August, when the heat and humidity hung motionless over our town. Everything stopped on those days. Nobody wanted to move. I sat in a chair in our living room, window open for the possibility of breeze, reading and sucking on ice cubes. In the dog days, I felt a peculiar kind of suspension, as if life had paused. No hurry. No rush. Even though I knew summer was almost over, and school would start again soon, I had plenty of time to savor the hush of those quiet, heat-hushed afternoons. If I read somewhere that "dog days" alludes to Sirius, the Dog Star, and its position in an August sky, I thought then, and I think now, of a large, lazy, floppy-eared dog, lying in the shade of a porch, patiently waiting out the heat.

After the dog days disappeared and the first chill of fall arrived, we could hope for a brief "Indian summer," those few warm days that unseasonably return and then disappear, all too quickly, back into the cold. As a child, I liked the faintly exotic sound of "Indian summer." Hinting at a shadowy past, those weather words connected me, in a vaguely romantic way, to the mythical people who had lived on these plains before us. I did not know much about Native Americans or why these rare days bore their name. (Paul Douglas says Indian summer might have been the time when Native Americans could complete their harvest.) I scarcely noticed Indian summer as it swiftly came and went.

Then, during my teenage years, a time when popular music seeps permanently into one's bones, Frank Sinatra re-recorded an old Tommy Dorsey hit called "Indian Summer." Its melancholy lyrics and slow, sad music recalled the ghost of a summer romance, fading too soon, and now forever vanished. Indian summer was here to watch over "some heart that is broken / By a word that somebody left unspoken," Sinatra crooned. Mourning the ending of love, the melody ended on a muted, drawn-out farewell. Hearing that poignant song made me feel, in what I thought of as a grown-up way, as if I were sensing the mysterious sadness that seemed to lurk at the heart of life.

So now, when someone remarks on a clear, sunny October day, "Looks like we're in for a little Indian summer," I don't immediately join in celebrating those few generous days of warm, sunny weather. Instead, as if I were thirteen or fourteen again, I am briefly overcome by an odd wistful feeling. Long-ago autumns whisper in my ear, with the faint echo of crackly leaves, brown heaps of them, raked from our yard into a blazing bonfire by the curb. Once, the Brayton boy down the block, ordinarily much too old to pay attention to me, came over to roast marshmallows in the embers. Indian summer: I hear it as a nostalgic melody, lingering in my mind after all these years, reminding me how quickly life passes—and, of course, how soon the weather changes.

Not surprisingly, since I am entranced by language, weather words, and the familiar images they convey, have become an unconscious part of my metaphorical vocabulary. Like many people, I lean on weather-related clichés like "a breath of fresh air" and "a ray of sunshine"; I feel a "chill blowing through me" from bad news; I apologize for a "gust of anger" or a "whirlwind of feelings"; I am glad to leave a crowded scene and escape "the eye of the storm." But I also can recall some pivotal times in my life when I found myself invoking an image from the weather to help me understand what was happening.

I remember, with a pang, the sunny, warm summer afternoon when, five years into my first marriage, I realized—for one moment—that I might someday get a divorce. I buried that realization instantly. But I never forgot it, and I thought of it in weather words. That may be why I came to see the end of our marriage in the metaphor of a storm. That moment occurred when I was sitting at a portable typing table, placed under a window in our spare bedroom, and working on my much-delayed doctoral dissertation. On that afternoon, I was deeply absorbed in my notes. Although I glanced up occasionally, looking out the window, I didn't really see anything.

Until I noticed Lawrence's little red car zoom up our hilly drive. I stopped typing immediately. What in the world was he doing home in the middle of the day? An ambitious young scientist, he spent long hours in his lab. Sometimes he did not come home until late at night. Now, as I watched, Lawrence reappeared at the side of the garage. He was walking fast toward the house, his head bent down, but his face visible—and I could tell he was angry.

I had learned to watch carefully for signs of impending rage. Besides a rising tone in his voice, I could recognize drawn brows and a darkness in his face. That was what I saw now. As I watched Lawrence march up the sidewalk, I knew something had made him so angry that he left work to come home and tell me about it. My quiet afternoon was about to be shattered, and I suddenly thought, to my horror, "Someday I will have to leave him."

Whenever, during the next few years, I let myself return to that moment, I remembered it in terms of weather. What I had seen out my window were the unmistakable signs of an approaching storm. That was part of what shocked me: I had viewed my husband, whom I loved, as a kind of unstoppable natural force beyond my power to alter or deflect.

I think of storms at happier times, too. When my grown daughter, Jennifer, comes home to visit, she arrives in a whirl of energy. Intense, emotional, and expressive, she radiates a kind of magnetic force field. Drawn into it, I find myself dashing here and there, driving, shopping, talking, enjoying my daughter's vivacity but barely keeping up to her speed. Her departure for the airport—all too soon—is usually filled with breathless injunctions ("Can you mail this?" "I forgot to check the dryer!" "Will you call this number?"). So when I go down to her empty bedroom and begin to move around it, picking up a dropped pencil or an orphaned sock, I stop dead in the middle of the floor. The room is so quiet. I can hear the wall clock ticking. This, I find myself thinking, is the proverbial calm after the storm. But oh, now that she's gone, I'm going to miss her.

My mind is a grab bag of weather words, aphorisms, and song lyrics. When I was in college, a "snow job" meant to bowl over, to wow, to bury someone with attention. When I've been swept away by someone's persuasive power, I still think, "Hey, I've been snowed!"

And for an instant I envision a dazzling rush of white snow smothering me under its drift. On rainy days, if I am feeling exuberant, I often find myself silently caroling, "I'm *sing*in' in the rain, just *sing*in' in the rain," a refrain that magnifies my high spirits. If I'm determined to get through something unpleasant, I'll tell myself to "weather it."

So much weather, so many metaphors. Those of us who live in the Midwest talk about the weather even when we don't think we are. Are you under pressure, we ask solicitously? Are you frozen into inaction? Is your heart melting? Can you sense a change in the air? What is happening outdoors? Indoors? Down deep in your soul? The weather we know so well tells us how to answer.

# Things That Go Buzz in the Night

> . . . but when the hot sun of summer had warmed them for a while
> they would suddenly burst open, letting loose a host of voracious,
> crawling devils.
>
> —O. E. Rolvaag, *Giants in the Earth*

My husband, james, does not understand why I do not always
love summer weather. But then he never gets bitten by bugs—
mosquitoes, yellow jackets, gnats, black flies, horse flies, and other,
unidentified pests who appear out of nowhere, strike, and disappear.
He walks across a meadow of ankle-high grass and remarks on the
breeze, the dark-blue sky, the beautiful evening. I walk beside him
and think of ticks and chiggers.

Everything bites me, everywhere. When I was a little girl, my
mother constantly had to daub Mercurochrome and Gentian Violet
(whose names were impressively medicinal) on the countless bites
I scratched until they bled and became infected. When I looked in a
mirror, I could see purple stains covering my face and arms like faded
war paint. When I was older, I swabbed my own bites with thick slimy
splotches of pink calamine lotion. I still itched. Eventually, despite
stoic resolve, I could not keep myself from scratching off the hardened

calamine like a scab. My childhood summers were months of carefree vacation, lazy hot afternoons—and angry red sores.

Now I operate on summer alert. Before I venture to my garden, even for a brief reconnaissance, I carefully prepare for war. On an open shelf in our bedroom, a tray of assorted repellents stands ready: spray, liquid, cream, cream with sunblock. It reminds me reassuringly of the tray of stainless sterile implements our family doctor used to keep on the shelf in his office. First I thoroughly spray my shirt, slacks, and socks. Then I rub gooey repellent into my face, ears, and neck. Ever since last summer, when a nasty winged thing crawled up under my shirt and bit me hard, causing deep red welts that lasted for ten days, I smear more repellent around my middle. As I walk outside, I move in an acrid haze of Deet.

How I envy people who can garden in shorts, T-shirts, and sandals. They look, if not cool, fairly comfortable, not to mention grubbily chic, in their stripped-down simplicity. Flying bugs would dive-bomb with glee if I were foolish enough to leave the house in anything less than shoes, socks, sturdy slacks, and long-sleeved shirt. As I lumber around the garden, I feel on hot days as if I'm encased in medieval armor, sweating Deet that stings as it runs into my eyes.

So after the first wonderful wet burst of spring, I get a little grouchy. Everyone else loudly rhapsodizes about what the hot weather promises—sunbathing, barbeques, boat rides, band concerts, bicycling, hiking, and camping. But I have begun to watch warily for the first mosquitoes. As soon as rain is followed by hot sunshine, I know they have hatched. Now they are poised out there, millions of them, hovering, waiting to pounce. It is only a matter of time until the first bite appears on my arm or ear or neck. I probably won't know when it happened. But suddenly I'll want to itch, and a swollen red spot will begin to rise, a tiny irritated mound, on my arm or earlobe.

Or maybe that bite isn't from a mosquito. I have sometimes slapped at other insects, wasplike creatures that aren't quite wasps, just as they've pierced my skin. I suppose I should buy an illustrated book of bugs so I could look them up. Then I could identify my enemies, learn about them, and resent them, in a more focused way, by their proper names. But I don't want to know them any better.

I feel guilty about this attitude. I understand that it shows a failure of curiosity, and, far worse, a lack of appreciation of God's creatures. When I am murderously contemplating a wasp's nest under our eaves, wondering how high I can aim a can of Raid, I think of one of my favorite novels, *A Passage to India*. In a short but significant scene, E. M. Forster shows how Mrs. Moore, an aging and almost saintly Englishwoman, reacts to a wasp perched on a peg where she wants to hang her cloak. Attuned to the spirit of India, Mrs. Moore regards the wasp with quiet admiration: "There he clung, asleep, while jackals in the plain bayed their desires and mingled with the percussions of drums. 'Pretty dear,' said Mrs. Moore to the wasp."

I know I should feel like Mrs. Moore. The Dalai Lama, I read somewhere, does not even slap mosquitoes—unless possibly, I think I remember, after several of his gentle reproaches, they persist in biting him. And I can't imagine that they seek him out. Only an overzealous, adolescent, ill-informed mosquito would ever want to cause pain to the Dalai Lama. It is not that I am deficient in awe for the unfathomable wonders of the created world. Several years ago, I spent an hour at the Chicago aquarium mesmerized by an exhibition about frogs. Tiny frogs, huge frogs, poisonous frogs, velvety frogs, bumpy frogs, jumping frogs, burrowing frogs, squat frogs, leggy frogs, brilliantly colorful frogs—I could never have dreamed up such a fascinating variety of frogs. If I were to study such an exhaustive exhibit of flies, or wasps, or mosquitoes—provided they were safely behind glass—I might feel differently about them. Maybe.

When I was eight or ten, my aversion to insects came to the attention of Mrs. Carew, a robust woman who organized the local troops of Camp Fire Girls. My troop leader must have confided to Mrs. Carew that I shrank from a bug-collecting badge. Maybe my mother spoke to Mrs. Carew, who was well known in Ames for her amateur scientific fervor, about my fear of spiders. So I visited Mrs. Carew, who, after lecturing me on foolish squeamishness, provided me with several Mason jars and a container of carbon tetrachloride. Mrs. Carew referred to it, with easy intimacy, as "carbon tet."

For a few weeks, I forced myself to pursue insects, instead of having them pursue me. I captured several skittery daddy longlegs, at least one dark small spider from a corner in our basement, and a few beetles I discovered here and there. I dutifully popped them all into a sealed jar holding a rag soaked with carbon tet, and then I remember some kind of mounting process, using a board on which I created an insect display. I showed my collection to Mrs. Carew. She was very pleased. "So we like bugs now, do we?" she boomed. I probably nodded. It was easier to lie.

I find it hard to reconcile biting insects with a spiritual view of the world. I know, viscerally, that they are an essential part of nature's plan, whatever that may turn out to be. I'm sure that if I were an entomologist, I would rejoice in their intricate design and complex adaptations. Even uninformed, I do realize that biting insects provide food for other, more immediately likable creatures—robins, say, or swallows. But it is difficult for me to believe in the beauty of gnats. I cannot quite get to the soul of gnats. When I walk around our city lake on a still summer afternoon, clouds of them follow me like a hellish halo. Once, during a routine visit to our doctor, I aggrievedly pointed out an inflamed ear. "Gnat bite, probably," he said calmly. He said it in the tone of someone dismissing something trivial, something utterly beneath notice, as metaphorically a mere gnat bite. Of course, it was not his ear that was swollen. Then he gave me an expensive cortisone ointment, which, I found, worked about on a par with Gentian Violet.

Although we close our outside doors quickly and keep our screened windows in good repair, a mosquito can float inside, just on the instant's breath between a door's opening and shutting. Then it waits. Later that night, after I've turned out my reading light, I begin to sink into sleep. Our bedroom windows are open to the mild air, and I sigh with pleasure at how balmy the night feels. Outside I can hear a faint rush of leaves in the breeze, a garage door opening and closing, a clicking of crickets. But just as I drift into darkness, I hear a faint droning buzz. It is a sound that anyone who has been outdoors in a Midwest summer can instantly recognize.

Now I am wide awake. Where is the mosquito? I turn on the bedside light. I look inside its small circle of brightness, and then I peer anxiously around the darkened room. Nothing. Then I turn off the light and hope that, against all odds, I won't hear the buzz again. But of course I do, and this time it is so close to my ear that I jerk upright. I imagine it hanging in midair like a miniature hummingbird, greedily surveying my face and neck, wondering where to land.

It is impossible to sleep if one is waiting for a mosquito to strike. James, who was a young tugboat captain in World War II, remembers listening and watching for buzz bombs in Belgium. "We'd lie awake in our bunks," he has told me, "and hear that sound. It really got on your nerves. You were all right as long as you could hear the buzz, because that meant the bomb, which was really a kind of rocket, was still in the air. But when the engine on the rocket cut out, the bomb would fall, right where it was. So when the sound stopped, especially if it was close, you didn't know whether in a few moments it would come down on top of you." Sometimes, as I wait, tensed, listening to a circling mosquito, I think of James, so many years ago, in his wartime bunk.

If the night feels early, I may heave myself out of bed, sleepily search for insect repellent, and then smear my arms, hands, neck, and face—any bit of temptingly exposed flesh. But I hate falling asleep to the smell of DEET. I imagine all that poison insidiously seeping into my lungs. Besides, I'll hear the mosquito darting, searching, testing. So usually I just pull the sheets around my head like a hood, leaving only a breathing hole for my nose. On an especially warm night, I can soon feel as if I'm in a slowly heating sauna.

As I lie in bed, I feel despairingly like the touchy heroine in the story of the princess and the pea. The princess, as any fairy-tale reader will remember, was so royally delicate that she could sense the hardness of an unsuspected pea under a high stack of mattresses. After one night atop the buried pea, she reported that she was exhausted. She hadn't slept a wink all night, and she was bruised black and blue. I am embarrassed to admit how a single hungry mosquito can so disturb my rest. I don't like to think of myself as an overly sensitive princess. But, when a mosquito threatens, that's what I am.

I ought to be ashamed. When I find myself fussing about mosquitoes, I remind myself about explorers in the early 1800s near Fort Snelling on the Minnesota River, not far from our Minneapolis home. Somewhere, years ago, I read a riveting historical account of how several of those young men were driven mad—literally, out of their minds, quite insane—by the hordes of mosquitoes that attacked them as they slept, defenseless, on the open ground. In *Bring Warm Clothes,* a wonderfully vivid anthology compiled from letters and photos at the Minnesota Historical Society, Peg Meier cites an only slightly less itch-making account by James E. Colhoun, who made an expedition to Minnesota in 1823. "Although I have a veil for the purpose, I find it necessary to keep a soldier constantly employed to brush away these troublesome insects while I am making Observations," he wrote, "& even with that aid I am seldom able to make them in a satisfactory manner." Not only men were troubled. "The horses crowd into the smoke of our fire," Colhoun added, "& several times have been so much distracted by stings of mosquitoes as to rush over our baggage & into the midst of the party."

So as I flap my hands around my head and curse, I think of those young adventurers, lying in a whirring, biting cloud of mosquitoes. Yes, undoubtedly I have it easy. In a modern Midwestern life with screens and Off!, mosquitoes, or indeed any biting insect, should not be a big deal. For most people, they *aren't* a big deal. Other travel writers, for instance. If I want to be particularly hard on myself, I'll think of travel writers I admire. I can claim only a self-deprecating kinship to most of them. In their resolute and tough-skinned company, I often feel as if I were a fluttery maiden aunt with dozens of well-muscled nephews. So many of them write with aplomb and panache about their harrowing adventures, including highly unpleasant confrontations with creepily threatening insects that would make a buzzing mosquito, or a dozen mosquitoes, seem totally insignificant.

Don't think of Tim Cahill, I tell myself. One of his books is called *Pass the Butterworms*. Don't remember Eric Hansen, who flicked scorpions away from his sleeping bag. Try not to call up the literary presence of Mary Morris. When she encounters insect pests in *Nothing to Declare*, she briskly deals with them and moves on. Here is how she contended with flying ants in Mexico: "I noticed the stucco walls around me, which were black and seemed to be moving. The molding of the window I faced was black and crawling. . . . I watched as Jerry swatted flying ants. Soon carcasses lay all over my floor. After the ants were killed, he sat down to talk." I would have been speechless.

I then begin to let my mind wander to other places, other bugs, other bites. Tropical islands, rural India, the South American jungle, the African plains. Suppose I lived among scorpions? Brown recluse spiders? Tsetse flies or malarial mosquitoes? Fire ants? (Just this morning I read a two-inch item, buried on the third page of the paper, about how an eighty-seven-year-old woman with Alzheimer's, lying in bed in a Florida nursing home, died of 1,792 bites from a swarm of fire ants. Or maybe it was 2,232. Someone had counted.)

As I swat at mosquitoes, I also pay silent homage to the pioneers, not to mention twentieth-century farmers. With the fairly recent development of powerful insecticides, Midwestern urban dwellers do not hear much anymore about the plagues of insects that used to devastate crops in the surrounding countryside. But for a hundred years or more, the Midwest's insects were a biblical threat. When I gloomily contemplate, on a merely personal level, a summer of bug bites, I try to remind myself of *Giants in the Earth*. Do I think I'm suffering? Ha! Think of Per Hans and his forlorn wife, Beret.

Although I read Ole Rölvaag's grim saga only once, that was enough to burn its bleak images into my mind. Toward the end of Rölvaag's novel, after he has shown the heartbreaking work necessary to establish a farm on the Midwestern prairie, he describes the arrival of locusts, which kept returning all during the 1870s: "On a certain bright, sunny day, when the breeze sighed its loveliest out of the northwest, strange clouds would appear in the western sky; swiftly they would advance, floating lazily through the clear air, a sight beautiful to behold. But these clouds would be made up of innumerable dark-brown bodies with slender legs, sailing on transparent wings; in an instant the air would be filled with nameless, unclean creatures— legions on legions of them, hosts without number! Now pity the fields that the hand of man had planted with so much care!"

Did I worry about a single mosquito? "It would happen for days at a time, during the height of the pest season, that one could not see clear sky." Sometimes the locusts would float by; "then, all of a sudden, as if overcome by their own neglect, they would swoop down, dashing and spreading out like an angry flood, slicing and shearing, cutting with greedy teeth, laying waste every foot of the field they lighted in." When the locusts' eggs hatched the next summer, "these little wriggling demons were not only revoltingly nasty to look at but they also caused an even greater devastation than those which came flying on the wings of the western breeze."

So an ordinary Midwest summer, with only mosquitoes and assorted other biters, should be seen in perspective. I'm sure it should. To be fair, on summer days when a brisk wind is blowing, I hardly notice bugs at all. Besides, the last time a yellow jacket stung me, my hand merely swelled a little, and I didn't go into anaphylactic shock, as I always fear I will. Yes, I acknowledge I am lucky not to have to worry about black widow spiders. Or giant cockroaches, or termites. And please notice that I always laugh, a little, when someone quips, yet once again, that the Minnesota mosquito ought to be celebrated as our state bird.

But I still lie awake, listening to the buzz.

# A Cold-Blooded Woman

High near 85. Current humidity 83 percent.

—Forecast, August 31, 2002

I CAN'T JUST BLAME THE BUGS. Something unpleasant happens to me in the peak of summer. For most of the year, I am a fairly reasonable woman. Oh, some days I can be rather irritable ("My service-tag number is 7GT68491, and my computer has just *crashed again!*"), and I certainly do snap occasionally ("You mean you invited them for dinner *tonight?*"). But I basically consider myself as settled and accepting—maybe not always calm, but, yes, mostly content and fairly reasonable.

As high summer approaches, I begin to change. Like a werewolf during a full moon, I turn into someone else. On the first day the temperature creeps above eighty, I start to mutter. "Eighty outside. Eighty already," I say to James over breakfast.

He pretends to ignore my tone. "Yes, it's a wonderful June day!" he says, returning from picking up the newspapers on the front steps. His cheerful disposition often makes me mutter louder.

"Oh sure," I say sourly, "except spring is definitely gone now. That'll be the end for the peonies. I'll bet we're going to have a really hot summer this year. The paper says it will get up to eighty-two today. Hah! I can tell it will be the mideighties at least. I'm going to have to turn on the air conditioner by noon."

James looks at me with a little pity. "Of course. Go ahead," he says benignly. This is a sacrifice, for he does not like air-conditioning. Some blistering afternoons, as I gratefully breathe artificially cooled air, I can see him sitting outside on our little terrace, steaming happily as he reads a book.

During a hot summer—and most summers lately have seemed to be unusually hot—I read the daily weather forecast with what I can only honestly describe as resentment. Hot again? Hotter? I hate this! Why can't we have a cool breeze now and then? A few days in the seventies? Is sixty-five an impossible dream? I find myself simmering, stewing, and coming to a boil, just like the weather outside. I have recently begun to wonder why this is so. I have lived here most of my life. I'm a grown-up. I know the facts. In the Midwest, winters are long and cold. Summers are hot. And short. So why have I not yet achieved a state of Zen tranquility?

I don't mind the cold of winter. Of course I grouse occasionally; what self-respecting Minnesotan doesn't? But, except for those rare years when snow continuously piles up, requiring daily shoveling, or when thick ice coats the pavement early and doesn't melt until spring, I regard winter with relative equanimity.

I used to feel that way about summer. When I was young, I actually liked the hottest days. Oiled with Coppertone, I flopped lazily on a blanket in our backyard as the sun baked and browned my almost-bare back. Some afternoons, barely dressed in a halter top and shorts, I bicycled around town, enjoying the warm breeze on my skin as I rolled along. When I could hang around the town's outdoor swimming pool, I looked forward to the delicious sensation of leaping from stingingly hot cement into ice-cold water.

But now the heat often feels to me like a heavy-handed bully. Grabbing me in an inescapable grip, it stuns me into inactivity. Lethargic, slow, I move as if in a deep-sea diving suit. I don't feel like cleaning, cooking, sorting laundry, paying bills, answering letters. I do not feel like returning phone calls. Or watering my garden. Most of all, I don't really feel like going outside. I'd turn beet red in the face; sweat would drip into my eyes; my feet would swell. I get headaches easily, and a long blast of July sun could trigger one. I've given up my estrogen, and hot flashes strike like lightning. Taking a blood-pressure medication that can exacerbate such reactions, I might feel a little faint. So not only won't I think about bicycling around town, I don't even want to walk.

This is serious. I depend on a daily three-mile outdoor walk to keep my spirits up and weight down. If I don't walk, I feel morose. Edgy. Not nice to be around. But in the heat, walking no longer feels like fun. On almost all winter days, I can bundle up and face the cold. In summer, aside from stripping, hosing myself down, and then heading naked out the door, I have never thought of a way to feel comfortable on an eighty-five-degree day in the sun. A sun hat doesn't do it. Nor do sundress, sandals, or a water bottle.

I have decided, fatalistically, that I probably have cold blood. Maybe, now that I'm older, it courses through my body at a few degrees chillier than normal. But unlike reptiles, I don't like to have it heated up. Half of my genetic inheritance is Norwegian, the other half an indeterminate mix of English and Scots. No one ever accuses these countries of scorching temperatures. Is that one reason I love to travel in the British Isles? Am I better adapted to rainy days, fall winds, cold nights?

But I can also think of a less comforting theory. I may resent summer heat because it is so inescapable. In January, I can keep warm. But in July, I can't stay cool. Summer is a hot sticky embrace; once I'm outside, I can't wiggle out of it. Tracing this resentment to its source, I might discover that I am struggling with—ah, I know this baggy monster well—control issues. Maybe, as I'm sure someone fluent in contemporary mantras would smugly tell me, midsummer heat is something I should regard as a valuable lesson. Let it be; accept; smile. A ninety-five-degree day? Eighty percent humidity? A dew point off the chart? Hey, another opportunity for personal growth!

So this summer I have resolved to change my attitude. I've been trying Norman Vincent Peale's old technique of the power of positive thinking. Steamy? Think languorous. Sizzling? Think crisp. Humid? Think balmy. Sweaty? Think cleansing perspiration. Hot, hot, hot? Stinking hot? Sweltering hot? Blistering, smothering, searing hot?

Well, there's the problem. Sometimes I bog down. I still feel hot. Then all I can do is stare for a while at the calendar. Now that I'm older, I also know that time passes fast. Far too fast. So I remind myself, with an unwelcome shiver, that fall—fresh, breezy, brisk, sparkling, cool fall—is just around the corner. And after fall comes winter. Far too fast. Sink back into summer, I tell myself. Make it last.

# Garden Weather

Awake, O north wind; and come, thou south; blow upon my garden.

—Song of Solomon 4:16

ON THE FIRST DAY OF SPRING, I am on my hands and knees in my garden. Like many Midwestern gardeners, I define spring not by a specific date on the calendar but by the weather. If I can dig in the dirt, spring has arrived. Sometime in April, even in March, winter's snow—gray, compacted, icy—will finally have melted. On several chilly days to come, a few flurries will whiten the ground, but they won't stay long. The deep stony frost has slowly, seepingly, imperceptibly made its way to the surface and disappeared. The heavy black soil in my garden is loose and friable, damp and fresh, easy to work. I can hardly wait to get my hands into it.

What I do on hands and knees is to celebrate, fervently if wordlessly, our survival. Mine, the garden's, something larger than both of us. Winters are hard, often brutally hard, on Midwestern gardens. (Summers aren't so easy, either.) Since I garden with abandon on the sprawling acreage surrounding our Wisconsin weekend house, I cannot cover all my plants in winter. For a few years I tried: in late fall I scattered bale after bale of hay over my shrubs and flower beds. But the wind blew much of it away, and I hated gathering the rest up, scratchy armful after armful, every spring. So I stopped.

Now, when headlines in our newspaper report a prolonged spell of subzero weather, accompanied by winds that depress the windchill temperatures to startling extremes (fifty, seventy below), I think of my naked garden. It lies there, unprotected, defenseless. Most of my plants, as I have seen from transplanting them, don't have roots deep enough to escape those probing fingers of icy cold. Others, I once read on their nursery tags, require special care during their first winter. Not yet hardened to their Midwestern life, they are as vulnerable as infants. I think of my new expensive daphne, two Japanese painted ferns, the Duchesse de Nemours wilted peony I rescued at an end-of-summer sale. I have abandoned them.

On the coldest days, I lie in bed in Minneapolis and think about my Wisconsin garden ninety miles south. Here in the city, on a small shaded urban lot, I only garden in pots. But what is happening right now outside our bluff-top cottage? Does the wind there bite as cruelly as outside my front door? I picture snow blowing over my hosta beds, covering the daylilies, burying the hardy shrub roses. At least, I hope they're hardy. During thaw-and-freeze, I look anxiously out my city window at the unexpected hailstorm, the driving sleet, the late-spring snow. I wonder if enough earlier drifts have lingered over the garden to provide some kind of insulating shield. Will the daffodils and emerging bleeding hearts die back to the ground? But if I were at the cottage, what could I do? I am no match for the weather.

Some years, as winter begins to ease, we have a sudden spell of warm days, followed by severe cold again. This, Midwestern gardeners know to their dismay, is a thaw-and-freeze cycle. It can doom plants that have been tricked into shaking themselves from their winter sleep, stirring again into green life, and sprouting their first stems or buds. A winter mulch would have saved them. I am sure they are lost.

So when that first spring day comes, I count each emerging plant as an unexpected miracle. And of course, it is. I begin to snap off dead stalks, scoop away fallen leaves, and pull mats of decayed foliage from the ground. There, hidden until now under a tangle of stalks, is a hearty favorite, five or six years old by now, a daylily called Dear Dad. Already it has poked a few inches of green above the dirt. Beneath the thatch of pine needles and brown leaves in my shade garden, I find Raspberry Splash, a new pulmonaria I tucked into a found space just before the killing frost last fall. Its green-and-white spotted leaves are happily curling upward. Raspberry Splash: the name sings of summer.

My garden is so big, unruly, and unkempt, that last spring I spent three long days, moving my cushiony kneeling pad from spot to spot, standing to unscrunch my muscles, then kneeling again, as I slowly uncovered each plant. I dashed inside every hour or so for a quick cup of tea, a bit of cheese or a slice of toast. Then back into the garden. At the end of three days, I could hardly walk, because my back and thighs felt as if someone had been relentlessly stretching them hour after hour. (Someone had.)

Mostly those three days were cloudy, with wisps of occasional snow, a shower of rain, a brief burst of hail. When the sun shone, I took off my jacket. My ears were cold, and my hands inside my canvas gloves, digging in the unfrozen dirt, were colder. But I had not been outdoors all day for months, and I thought the weather was wonderful.

As I moved, awkwardly and sometimes painfully, from one patch of ground to another, I began reacquainting myself with what was growing there. When I began this Wisconsin garden, I realized after the first season or two that I needed plant labels. Otherwise, over the winter, I forgot where everything was, and I inadvertently dug up old plants when I started to plant new ones. Or something would begin to grow, and I would then puzzle for weeks over what it was. So now, unsightly as they are, small metal labels on wire legs announce the name of each plant. In spring, before greenery dwarfs them, the labels look like a tiny metal forest.

But I know I am growing more than galvanized steel and zinc. As I unveil each hopeful green shoot, brushing away debris and clearing the soil, I look at it fondly. "Tukie's peony!" I say quietly to myself—often, in fact, quite aloud, since no one is around to hear. My friend Tukie told me what it was when she gave it to me, but I forgot, so I just named it after her. *Cimicifuga racemosa!* I remind myself, greeting the stubbly beginnings of what I know will quickly grow into four-foot, airily waving fronds. I am not a purist about nomenclature. I put down whichever name, Latin or common, I happen to like best. *Cimicifuga racemosa* sounds niftier than "bugbane," just as "false dragonhead" is pleasanter than "phystostegia," a tongue twister that suggests a plodding dinosaur. Since Dear Dad is perfect for a faithful old daylily, I don't bother to add *Hemerocallis* on its plant label. After all, we're on a first-name basis.

So in early spring, I call the roll. Yes, we are all survivors. Here I am again, still able to wield a spade, ready to tackle a garden that I know already—that I knew last year, and the year before that—is far too big for one not-so-young, busy woman to handle by herself on short visits and weekends. But I cannot bring myself to hack it down to a manageable size. To make it smaller, I would have to dig up some plants and—well, there's no other way to put it—kill them. Nobody I know wants any of them. I don't grow anything exotic enough to interest most experienced gardeners.

The compost heap is a good idea. But as I look at all these sturdy, determined shoots in spring, I marvel at their tenacity. I didn't offer protection; they suffered the worst of winter; yet here they are. How could I now destroy them? I look somewhat dispiritedly at my two globe thistles. I put them into the middle of my garden years ago, when I was experimenting to see what would thrive in a particular semishady spot. After a few seasons, discouraged by lack of sun, heavy clay soil, and hooves of wandering deer, many plants gave up. No more coreopsis, or baby's breath, or foxglove.

But the globe thistles prospered. By midsummer, their gray-green prickly leaves towered triumphantly over surrounding daylilies. The problem was that I didn't like them much. When I studied the colored photograph at the nursery, I had envisioned brilliant blue flowers contrasting pleasantly with gold and yellow daylilies. Instead I got lots of untouchable foliage and a few faded, almost unnoticeable pale-blue blooms. Globe thistle unfortunately looked too much like its close relative, a common weed.

Yet year after year, my globe thistles continue to perform. Each fall, as they finally droop from frost, I say to myself sternly, "That's it. Next spring, out they go. I'll make room for something else." But then in spring, I see how confidently and assertively the thistles push out of the cold damp soil. So they're not particularly pretty, I tell myself. They made it through the winter. I guess I owe them.

In early spring, before the gnats or mosquitoes or bees arrive, I love working in my garden. On those bugless, cool days, anything seems possible. I see each tiny shoot as the dazzling flower it will soon become. Weeds are not yet a problem, if I ignore the infinite strings of creeping Charlie that have threaded themselves through every square inch of unoccupied soil. So I am free to imagine the summer of my dreams. This year the rabbits won't eat my tulips, and the deer won't relentlessly gnaw each twig of my Nippon blue hydrangea. Cutworms won't turn my hollyhock leaves into lacy figments. My monarda will not wilt with fungal mildew. My Carefree Beauty rose, given to black spot, will actually turn out to be carefree. Yes, this summer the garden will be flawless, with one wave of bloom following another, until it peacefully subsides into the first frost of fall.

Of course I know that I am dreaming. But a Midwestern spring is full of hope. It encourages belief. For someone like me, who tends to look warily ahead, it insists that I stop, plopped on my muddy knees, and savor each moment. For gardeners know that this glorious weather—clear blue mornings, warming breezes, cool sunshine—is all too brief. Soon another front will blow it away. Winter was cold, summer will be hot. Now, in early spring, we are granted a few days of respite, a chance to stretch and breathe deeply. A tiny clump of delicate white Dutchman's-breeches trembles beneath a prickly ash tree. Look at it, enjoy it, because it will soon be gone.

Garden weather teaches a Midwesterner dramatic lessons not only about survival but also about change. Yes, all things change. I already knew that. As a graduate student, I read through pages, volumes, centuries of plays and poems musing over mutability. Nothing stays the same, the wheel turns, the goddess changes her mind. No one knows what will happen next. Count on nothing, except, depending upon the writer, on God, or art, or love, or change itself. And love, they mostly agreed, wasn't a sure thing. But when I was in my twenties, I did not want to believe in impermanence.

On a June evening in my first garden, I learned. When Lawrence and I bought a house, I was eager to try gardening. Since I had never grown anything except indoor plants, I knew nothing about how to start. During the winter, I sent for nursery and seed catalogs, as my mother had always done. As a child, I had pored over the alluring pictures in the thick Gurney's catalog. Smug customers sent in many of them, slightly blurred black-and-white snapshots of astonishing successes. Here was a mammoth zucchini, larger than its proud owner's arm. There was a woman standing among dahlias (or zinnias, or sweet peas) shooting toward the sky. This man's marigold, held triumphantly aloft, had won Best of Show at the North Dakota State Fair. Order any of these, Gurney's magnanimously promised, and they would also throw in a mystery plant. Whatever it is, it will grow! And who knows? Maybe you too will be a winner!

I was hooked. Besides packets of seeds, I ordered many live plants, mostly ones I thought I could recall from my mother's old-fashioned garden: delphinium, phlox, hollyhock. Lawrence agreed to dig up a square of lawn I had staked out in our backyard. But my potentially prize-winning plants arrived too soon. According to the Gurney's calendar, spring was supposed to be here. Actually, it had come. Only now it had left again. Following several days of warm, sunny weather, a cold front blew in from Canada. Fronts, as Midwesterners learn, are often sharp-edged, and this one was like the giant blade of a celestial snow shoveler, relentlessly pushing its weather forward.

So I had to put my package of tender plants in our garage. By the time the unseasonable snow had melted and I had been able to return to my square of turned-over earth, the bits of green had developed a dispiriting grayish mold. I planted them anyway. But I had not realized that because my new garden was directly under a large tree, the emerging canopy of leaves would keep the sun from warming whatever flickering life might have been left. Everything quickly died.

On a little hill above us, our next-door neighbor, Mr. Willits, a gentle older man long retired from everything but gardening, had been watching. Now, from over his side of the hedge, he tentatively, unobtrusively offered advice. Why not plant something near the back door, around the large boulder that no one had ever bothered to remove from that sunny corner of lawn? The boulder was a focal point, he said, and besides, it would reflect heat and shelter my flowers. Put in lots of peat moss first, he said, keep watering, and everything will be fine.

He was mostly right. Or, rather, he was totally right, except for the weather. This time, again advised by Mr. Willits, I went to a local nursery and bought plants I could put into the ground that same day. I dug in pails of peat moss. I watered, tested the soil for dryness each day, watered again. Finally, as spring turned into full summer, I could see that I had a garden. It was not large—some petunias, daisies, and just one impressive delphinium, with sky-blue cupped petals on a surprisingly tall stem. I walked around the big boulder, admiring my plantings from every angle. Proud and happy, I called Lawrence from the house so he could see just how the white daisies set off that vivid blue delphinium. Over the hedge, Mr. Willits applauded. At last, I was a gardener.

I remember that night so well because, just after midnight, a new front blew in. Thunder, lightning, heavy winds, rain. Sometimes I tell myself that was the storm of all storms, the one in which Lawrence warned me, as I cowered in the basement, that our house would soon shatter above us. But really, it probably wasn't. Sudden severe storms are common in June. What I do know is what I saw next morning. As soon as I got up, I grabbed my bathrobe and hurried out to check on my garden. When I had gone to bed, I had sunk contentedly into sleep with the memory of those proudly flowering plants.

Now it was no longer a garden. High winds and heavy rains had flattened the petunias. Most of the daisies were crumpled, too. Maybe they would recover. But my delphinium wouldn't. The wind had snapped its stem, and it sprawled, already half-wilted, on the rain-soaked ground. As far as my little garden was concerned, the season was already over. It was only the end of June.

Although I have had, over the intervening years, many garden disasters, this is the one that prepared me for all the others. Though not unkindly, Lawrence said he couldn't understand why I was so upset. He saw a few smashed flowers and broken stalks; I saw the torn and ripped canvas of a living painting. But I had been taught an unforgettable lesson. For one brief warm evening, everything had been flawless. When I woke up, it wasn't. Weather changes, and that's that.

So now, many years later, from the first glimmering anemones to the last lingering yellow-gold chrysanthemum, I try to remember to notice it all. As best I can, I pay attention. Each evening at our cottage, James and I walk slowly around my garden. James is no gardener. He hates grubbing in the dirt, transplanting, weeding. In fact, if I press him into service, he is apt—by mistake, of course—to uproot the wrong plant. Once he applied fertilizer from a container holding traces of poisonous herbicide. But I forgive him, because he loves the garden. He has an important role in it, I tell him. He appreciates.

As we pass each fresh bloom of the day, I point it out. This, I say, is my new hosta, Citation. Can he see what a luminous apple green its leaves are? How creamy the edges? Carefully holding a glass of wine left over from supper, he leans close, and nods. We walk to a daylily that has opened today for the first time. Now this, I point out, is Flaming Poppa. Great name, he agrees. Look, I add, how its deep red petals sink into a green heart. We stand for a few moments and admire it.

"You know," James says, as we stroll further, "I don't think we should forget those beautiful little blue flowers." He waves a hand at the myosotis, a forget-me-not that spreads irresistibly over my garden. Some gardeners think of forget-me-nots as mere ground cover. They are so easy to grow that I often take them for granted. James makes sure I don't. He stoops to pick one of them, and we both examine it. I had forgotten how each tiny jewellike blue flower also has a dot of yellow and white, perceptible only if you look very closely.

The myosotis blooms into the heat of summer, just as I begin to fade. After the exaltation of spring, summer all too soon turns my garden into something more challenging. Laying siege to the garden, extreme weather tries one tactic, then another. One year, rain fell most of May and June. Rain, rain, more rain. My clay soil slurped and soaked it up until it could hold no more. Then little ponds formed here and there among the flower beds. One afternoon, during a brief letup, I dug a large hole intended for a new rosebush. Next morning, the hole was filled with water. I waited a few hours. The water refused to go down. I waited another day. Still the hole looked like a brimful bucket stuck in the ground. Not for two weeks did most of the water, quarter inch by quarter inch, gradually disappear. The whole garden smelled of mud.

Another summer we had a drought—weeks and weeks without more than the faintest sprinkling of rain. Lawns turned brown, leaves fell from the trees, farmers despaired. Everywhere—post office, shops, buses—people talked about the drought. They looked at the sky, examined every white cloud, and then shook their heads. An ominous feeling pervaded the city. I began to wonder, knowing I was foolish, if rain might never come again. Would the world ever be green once more? Or would everything just dry up and blow away?

That summer of drought I felt as if I were fighting for the very life of my garden. It was me against the weather. All I had was a hose. Every weekend, as we arrived at our cabin, I hurried from the car to the outside spigot and turned on the sprinkler. Hour by hour I moved it from one part of the garden to another, but I could never soak the soil quite enough before we had to leave again. During the week, my plants baked alone in the hot sun. In the winter I had thought of their cold roots; now I imagined those parched roots shriveling and dying.

One day, as summer drifted toward fall, rain—heavy, drenching, life-giving—finally fell. My stepdaughter Lucy, who is now a gardener herself, told us that she was driving out of town when she saw the clouds break. She pulled off the road, got out of the car, and danced in the downpour until she was soaking wet. If I had been in my garden, I like to think I would have danced too.

Although I can fight drought with a hose drawing on a deep well, I can't do anything about the heat. Some midsummer days, when I am soaked, sticky, and a little woozy, I ask myself: Why am I doing this?

Coming here for only a few days at a time, I can't possibly pinch dead blooms, spray for fungus before it spreads, or notice black spot in its earliest stealthy approach. I'll never get the garden free of weeds. I can only conduct a kind of holding action, a trench warfare that will keep my garden from being overwhelmed completely.

My opponent is formidable. All I have to do is glance at the edges of the garden. A few months ago, I could look through the bare woods to a dry creek bed. Now an impenetrable green wall presses against my border of mown grass. Beneath the trees, advancing fearlessly after each attack, is another low forest of weeds, many three or four feet high. Something is out there, breathing heavily, a warm moist blast that whispers, *"Grow! Grow!"*

When I studied art history in college, I was fascinated by the ancient figures of fertility goddesses from prehistoric Mediterranean and Near Eastern cultures. Although they had burgeoning breasts, many of these goddesses were surprisingly thin, wasp-waisted with slender arms. If I had a sculptor's gift, I would fashion a very different kind of image. In a Midwest summer, I imagine a huge earth mother, someone with lots of flesh, the kind of older, ponderously moving woman who wears an apron and emerges from a kitchen filled with alluring yeasty smells. Damp and perspiring, she holds out her arms to enfold everything in her reach. Her embrace can be smothering, but she reeks of life.

That is the kind of goddess who is urging my garden forward. By mid-July, I can easily see that it is not under my control. Yes, I can water. I can weed. But something powerful is making these plants grow—and not just grow, but explode into maturity—with a kind of frantic energy that is close to concentrated fury. *"Grow! Grow! You have only a few more weeks! Do what you can! Time is short! Winter is coming! Grow! Grow!"*

Anyone from the rural Midwest knows the saying "You can hear the corn growing in the night." Although as a young teenager I worked many weeks on a detasseling crew, I have never spent a night close enough to a cornfield to test this theory. But sometimes, when I walk near our Wisconsin cottage on a hot, shimmery midsummer evening,

I pass along a quiet road lined by cornfields. As I listen to the gentle rustle and crackle of the cornstalks in a humid breeze so slight it does not reach the road, I wonder if I can indeed hear them inching upward with unstoppable determination. They too must hear that voice: *"Grow! Grow!"*

Those hot summer days do offer their own special gifts. If someone hears me complain about the weather in late July or August and asks, "So why aren't you in England?" I can reply, as a kind of shorthand, "Corn on the cob and ripe tomatoes." If my questioner has spent any time in the Midwest, he or she will nod understandingly.

Although I don't grow vegetables in my weekend garden—too many rabbits and deer—I eagerly await the roadside stands that spring up in late July as quickly as growing corn. Their unevenly hand-lettered cardboard signs proclaim "Sweet Corn! Tomatoes!" Last summer, as we drove down the main street of a small Wisconsin town, I spotted our first sign. "Local corn!" I yelled, and James screeched to a stop next to the roadside folding table.

Rinsed in their husks, microwaved for a few minutes, and then peeled and lightly slathered with butter and a little salt, those pale yellow nuggets of sweet corn were young and tender. They didn't crunch; they almost dissolved. Midwest lore says that the best-tasting sweet corn is picked and then boiled within minutes, so the corn sugars are pulsing with life. That ambrosial treat still awaits me, and if I spent my summers in England (where corn on the cob is nearly nonexistent), I would never have a chance at it.

Most gardeners in temperate climates can grow tomatoes. I like English tomatoes, which have solid little bodies, firm texture, and a no-nonsense, orangey sort of taste. I've had excellent tomatoes, with a mellow or sharp tang, in countries as different as France and Crete. But only in the Midwest, in mid to late August for a few short weeks, can I find big, juicy, glowingly red tomatoes ripened by long afternoons under a steaming summer sun. These are not necessarily tomatoes to add pungency to red sauce, or tomatoes for a winey-dark stew. Their flavor is too delicate, their juiciness too sweet.

Once, when I stopped to visit a friend near lunchtime one late August, she asked if I'd like to stay for a tomato sandwich. Stepping outside to her garden, she brought two large ripe tomatoes to her cutting board. "They're warm from the sun," she said, caressing them for a moment. When she sliced them, they fell apart, but she managed to scoop them onto two slices of toast brushed with a little olive oil. She added a few fresh green leaves of basil; by August, it has flourished too. "It's awfully hot today," she said equably, biting into the sandwich. I had to dab at the juice running down my chin before I could answer with equal cheerfulness. For once, I wasn't about to complain of summer weather: I was savoring its taste.

I am not always comfortable in Midwest summers, but I can surprise myself by reveling in their intensity, their fierceness, and their brash colors. Not long ago, James and I celebrated my birthday with a ten-day midsummer trip to England. In Suffolk, we drove one afternoon to Helmingham Hall, where a moated Tudor country house is surrounded by immaculately kept grounds and gardens. Among them is a huge walled garden, and I sat on a bench for a while, awash in color, as I turned from side to side to admire the effect of lavish pale pink and coral shrub roses spreading against rosy-red brick, its color softened by age. Tall sprigs of lavender and creamy blossoms of London Pride added their own harmonious pastel notes. I was flat-out envious.

When I walked two weeks later into my own Wisconsin garden, I laughed out loud—mostly out of pleasure, and also at a remembered comparison. My garden, of course, now boasted a healthy assortment of two-foot-high weeds. But it also sang, loudly and brassily, in its own key. Beds of shocking orange tiger lilies waved like signal flags, accented by hybrid daylilies in gold, red, and lemon yellow. Tall purple coneflowers, yellow-and-brown daisies, and gold and rose-red achillea rose in clumps here and there. My vibrantly green hostas were now enormous, as much as four feet across, and their wandlike lavender and white flowers waved in the wind. All of this had happened in the brief time I'd been gone.

This, I thought to myself, messy and rambling as it is, looks just as beautiful—well, almost as beautiful—as Helmingham Hall. The

English garden will last for weeks, its blooms lingering in cool rainy weather, and then the pastel shades will gently, oh so slowly, fade. But the exuberant vigor of my own garden is as brief as a trumpet blast. My daylilies will soon drop their blossoms, the coneflowers will wilt, and soon the chrysanthemums, my last celebrants, will turn brown. By mid-September, we just might have a killing frost. All this glory, all this clamor, produced in just seven or eight weeks. Seven or eight weeks more, and—whoosh—everything is gone.

"Don't you wish you lived in England so you could garden year round?" a friend once asked me, looking over my ever-expanding beds. Well, no. When the frost arrives, I am ready. In fact, I am worn out. I am tired of weeding, of battling mosquitoes and gnats, of trying to keep up with that relentless pace. *("Grow! Grow!")* My gardening energies have petered out, just as my plants have begun to droop and shrivel. I am now thinking wistfully of chilly afternoons in front of the fire, a book in my hand and a cat on my lap.

But garden weather doesn't end with that first frost. Always in a race with the first snowfall, I find myself each fall outdoors on one particularly cold, windy day, holding a bag of daffodil bulbs, twenty-five, fifty, however many whose glowing, lemon-yellow or sun-gold photographs I could not resist as I browsed down the aisle of the garden store. I've been traveling, I've been writing, I've been procrastinating. Now, before winter slams the door, I have to get these bulbs into the ground.

Once, when my daughter saw me, woolly hat jammed over my ears, heavy gloves on my hands, muddy shoes, as I began digging holes for my daffs, she looked puzzled. "But why, Mom?" Jennifer asked. "You've got plenty of daffodils already." She is not a gardener yet, so she doesn't understand. There are never enough daffodils. I plant these bulbs with a kind of defiant assertion: they will make it through the winter, I will make it through the winter.

Every fall, when I am planting those late bulbs, I think of Katharine White, editor, garden columnist, and wife of the extraordinary writer E. B. White. After her death, E. B. White edited an anthology of his wife's essays, *Onward and Upward in the Garden*. In a moving foreword, he described how, just months before she died, Katharine White sat in her garden, directing the planting of bulbs: "As the years went by and age overtook her, there was something comical yet touching in her bedraggled appearance on this awesome occasion—the small, hunched-over figure, her studied absorption in the implausible notion that there would be yet another spring, oblivious to the ending of her own days, which she knew perfectly well was near at hand, sitting there with her detailed chart under those dark skies in the dying October, calmly plotting the resurrection."

Although Katharine White gardened in Maine, not the Midwest, she knew about difficult weather. But difficult weather can also be garden weather. As I think of her bent but indomitable figure, I dig another hole in the cold dark soil. Sprinkle a little bone meal, settle the bulb, mix peat moss and compost together, cover the bulb firmly. Another daffodil, ten to go. Moving to the next open space, I shiver a little but tell myself, "Garden while you can." Keep going until winter. Then wait. Spring will come.

# The Weather Doesn't Grow Old

weather (v. tr.) 1. To expose to the action of the elements, as for dry-
ing, seasoning, or coloring. 2. To discolor, disintegrate, wear, or otherwise affect adversely by exposure. 3. To come through (something)
safely; survive *(weather a crisis).*

—*The American Heritage Dictionary*

MOST MORNINGS I AM A LITTLE GROGGY when I wake up, so
when I sit down for breakfast, with my husband already deep into the
editorial page of the *New York Times,* I reach for the local newspaper
and turn immediately to the back page of the Metro section, where I
can find the weather report. As I sip a mug of steaming-hot tea, I concentrate intensely on temperature, yesterday's weather, and today's
predicted highs and lows, and slowly the morning begins to come
into focus.

"Upper eighties today," I announce with disapproval. James mur-
murs a noncommittal "Really?" Or I might inform him grimly, "Hey,
the high won't even get to the teens again! And we've got a 40 percent
chance of snow by tonight." He half-listens, his interest mildly piqued
but certainly not engaged. Even if I proclaim "Thunderstorms tonight!
Possible tornadoes!"—my shocked tone demanding a response—
James nods and accepts it with equanimity. He returns to Maureen
Dowd. I go back to the weather page.

I am not sure why, as I've grown older, I have become increasingly addicted to weather reports. I am determined to know, in advance, what the day promises: heat, cold, rain, ice, wind, frost, or sticky humidity. As I drink my tea and brood over the forecast, I may be trying to protect myself. In a complicated and uncertain world—I am finally old enough to realize most things are beyond my control—I like to think at least I have some assurance about each day's weather.

I am not the only one who takes forecasts personally. One especially warm afternoon this summer, driving home from our Wisconsin weekend cottage, James and I stopped in a small town to buy some homegrown vegetables. The farmer, a graying, beefy man, had parked his pickup outside a gas station. As he sorted through the heap in his truck for six unblemished ears of corn, I said casually, "It's turned out hot today, hasn't it?"

"Yup," he agreed. He continued ripping husks and tossing ears back.

"Wasn't supposed to get this hot," I commented companionably.

"Nope," he replied, and then added, sounding downright fierce, "but then they never get it right, do they?" He dropped three ears into a paper sack.

Now we were having a real conversation. "You know," I went on, "have you ever noticed that in the summer when they say it's going to be eighty, it always turns out to be eighty-five or ninety? And in winter, they tell you it'll be fifteen above, and it ends up five below. Or they predict light snow, and we get ten, twelve inches."

He stopped picking through the corn and looked at me sternly. "You've got it," he said. "That's the way it always is."

"So why," I asked, "do you think that is?"

He didn't hesitate. "Oh, I know," he said sourly. "They do it because of business. That's it. Business. They're all in cahoots." He shoved my last ear into the sack. I took two dollars out of my billfold, thanked him, and walked back to our car.

As we drove away, I wished I'd asked why, for what reasons, scheming forecasters would skew their weather predictions for "business." Who could possibly profit from forecasts too low or too high? But the more I thought about our brief exchange, the more I came to believe that we had actually been talking about belief. The fate of his crops was always and forever in the hands of a climate so unpredictable, changeable, and frequently destructive that it defied all attempts to soften some of its blows. Acolytes of inscrutable weather, forecasters had to be in cahoots with something equally malevolent and mysterious: "business." Better "business," I supposed, than God.

But clearly I too harbored my own conspiracy theory. I always regarded weather forecasters as incurably optimistic. Of course, I figured, they probably knew, deep down, that an eighty-degree day would heat up to an uncomfortable eighty-five or ninety. But they didn't want to admit it. Let everyone adjust to eighty, don't scare them with eighty-five or ninety, they told each other.

Or perhaps the temperature is plummeting? "Surely it won't go past five below!" they say to themselves. And a few degrees shouldn't matter to anybody, right? Five? Ten? What's the diff? Like a restive adolescent, I had decided that forecasters act like overprotective parents. Don't they think we are grown-ups out here? Can't we handle the truth? Why do "they" keep us from knowing what is really going to happen? And who are "they," anyway? Was the farmer right? Are "they" all in cahoots?

As I pursued this ludicrous line of thinking, I had a weird inspiration. Perhaps I should tabulate, in a cool and rational way, the difference between predicted and actual weather over one summer and one winter. I'd nail 'em! But of course, imagining myself at the breakfast table with my lengthening chart of statistics, I could also quite accurately imagine James's hoots of laughter. After a moment's reflection, I felt silly about the idea myself.

This kind of personal intensity about forecasts—not to mention paranoia about forecasters—has crept up on me. I can't remember if I read a weather bulletin very often when I was growing up. I must have checked occasionally to see, for example, whether rain might spoil the all-night prom picnic or a blizzard prevent our driving to the state basketball tournament. Mostly I didn't care about forecasts. But now that I am older, I have some new habits. I no longer pay attention to many things—*Vogue,* the Oscars, crabgrass, dinner parties for eight—but I do pay attention to the weather.

The weather, I have happily discovered, does not grow old. Everything else does. Naturally I refused to believe in aging when I was young. But now I do. I am aware that the tall cherry tree where my father once lifted me into white blossoming branches has long since been cut down. My mother, once quick of wit and sharp of tongue, sits smiling, but speechless and unknowing, in the nursing-care section of her retirement home. A childhood friend has colon cancer. Another struggles with diabetes. I look in the mirror at a body that sometimes startles me, its neck wrinkling, waist thickening, breasts drooping. When I find by chance a snapshot of myself just ten years ago, I am amazed at how young I was then.

So I take comfort in the continuing freshness, the unforeseen newness, of weather. The seasons always return with the startling impact of an exciting discovery. When the first warm spring breeze blows through my frozen garden, I am almost giddy with delight. I had forgotten how it feels to walk outdoors with only a light jacket, feeling a light tingle of pleasurable chill that slowly disappears in the mild spring sunshine. Later that night, a gentle rain begins to fall, and I can almost hear the last encrusted patches of dirty snow melting under the eaves. Tomorrow I may be able to see the green tips of crocuses pushing through the dark wet soil. None of this feels like last year's spring, a spring fading and aged, on its way out the door into oblivion. I am meeting it for the first time.

As I've grown older, summers seem to have grown hotter, stronger, more insistent. Each July, as I tuck paper towel into the band of my gardening hat, in a futile attempt to absorb the sweat that begins to drip down my face minutes after I dig my first bucket of weeds, I think with amazement: "This is so *hot!*" Summer slams into the Midwest with pent-up energy. I think sometimes of a painting—or have I painted this image into my mind from some ancient myth I once read?—in which a glowing sun god, bright shooting streaks around his head, strides across the canvas. Each year this sun god is young, robust, irrepressible.

Autumn is a familiar metaphor for inevitable decay. I cannot ignore how everything green and growing begins to brown, curl up, and die. Yes, I have my melancholy days in autumn. But I also think of this season as revitalizing. Just as I love the first balmy air that wafts into my spring garden, I welcome the clear, shivery wind that blows away the last humid haze of summer. It has a clean sharp sweep to it, knocking down faded blooms, stripping trees back to their spiky bones, and whisking dead leaves into the air. After the lassitude of summer's hot days, I feel a surge of fresh energy.

When the first heavy snow falls in winter, it is so white, so brilliantly pure, so quietly insistent about softening every harsh angle and healing every eyesore, that it always astonishes me. I remember how beautiful winter can be. That first snowfall arrives with breathtaking innocence. Who needs to wait until New Year's Eve for an opportunity to start life all over again? The snow lies just outside one's window, unmarked.

Not only do Midwest seasons regularly return—though not usually when expected—with the sparkling assurance of young wild children, each day always remains a surprise. Often the weather offers a one-day roller-coaster ride, a jarring rush downward, a sudden steep ascent, or both. Is it hot and stuffy in the morning, with sticky vapor as visible as a steam bath? By late afternoon, a thunderstorm may have cooled the air so quickly that I have to grab a light sweater for my walk. Open windows, shut windows. Fan on, fan off. In one day I may turn on the furnace in the morning, the air conditioner in late afternoon. In fall, I have learned to be wary of putting a big pot of soup on the back step to cool overnight. The temperature could fall twenty or thirty degrees without much warning, and next morning I might find myself trying to decant chunks of ice.

Mostly I know what to expect when I leave the house in the morning, but I can never be quite sure. Perhaps I wouldn't really like to know. If research meteorologists—I like the fact that the root Greek word, *meteorologia*, means "discussion of astronomical phenomena," with its implied mysteries—really did discover how to predict with infallible accuracy, I would probably not be so happy with them either. I think I'm glad the weather still catches me by surprise. Otherwise, I might begin to feel really old.

# Who Speaks in the Pillar of Cloud?

> We had the sky, up there, all speckled with stars, and we used to lay on
> our backs and look up at them, and discuss about whether they was
> made, or only just happened.
>
> —Mark Twain, *Huckleberry Finn*

I CANNOT IMAGINE living in the midst of Midwest weather
without sometimes thinking about God—or at least about a mysterious Power in the universe. When black thunderclouds overwhelm
the sun and crackling bolts of electricity split the darkness, I do not
immediately consider the facts of meteorology. I feel instead a tremor
of fear, tinged with awe. Wandering around under an unsettled sky,
Midwesterners constantly confront our puniness. A wind that whips
and whirls sleet like a lash, a blowing snowstorm that wipes out the
world, a sun that relentlessly dissolves solid asphalt: who can watch
all this and not wonder?

Wonder does not always lead to adoration. Our weather blasts us
with questions about love and justice that are impossible to answer.
As I stare at front-page photographs of a tornado's wake, a trailer park
strewn with debris, or a small town reduced to kindling—four dead,
forty injured, hundreds homeless—I see undeniable evidence of ter-
rifyingly random devastation. Floods, blinding blizzards, murderous

cold, lethal heat waves, lightning-sparked fires: every year our weather wreaks its havoc.

Yet our weather brings its miracles, too. On the first thawing day of spring, Midwesterners rush outside, crowding sidewalks and parks, rolling down car windows, basking in the sunshine on our uncovered heads. We smile at strangers, ready, all of us, to take to our hearts this lighthearted guest who will probably not be staying long. Spring's first visit is merely a flirtation, a tease. Still, we are reassured. Spring will come again. If I could soar over the city with the right kind of sensor on that day, I would hear a long intake of breath and then the thud of thousands of heavy coats falling from shoulders. If everyone went to daily services, this would be a morning we sang hymns.

Although we no longer hear the voice of preachers like Jonathan Edwards, the eighteenth-century Massachusetts pastor who famously thundered about sinners in the hands of an angry God, we cannot escape the voice of weather. I suspect it may possibly provoke scoffers into an intuitive spiritual response. When I was a freshman in college, my English teacher assigned us William James's *The Varieties of Religious Experience.* Although I plowed through these psychological essays, I have to admit that I remember little of them. But I have never forgotten his probing and open-ended title. I consider it one way of describing how we live, day by day, in Midwest weather: an immersion in the varieties of religious experience.

Not all Midwesterners claim to think about God, but they definitely think a lot about the weather. Listen, for example, to how we constantly, anxiously, and obsessively talk about it. "So what do you think of this weather?" we ask each other every day. The sales clerk who wraps my package inquires, "How is it out there?" She may ask the next customer, and the one after that. The boy who carries my groceries to my car, the woman who sinks into the bus seat next to me, the friend who calls to arrange lunch: they all want to comment on the weather.

The mailman sloshes up to my door and calls out with resigned humor, "Wet enough for you?" This is only his first verse. Another morning, he might move on to "Nice day for ducks!" In high summer, he may add, "We sure needed this!" and in April or September, "We don't need any more of this, do we?" What we need, or don't need, is a suggestive litany, implying, I think, that some ineffable authority has an interest in providing for—or ignoring—our desires. "We sure needed this!" sounds grateful; "we don't need any more," resentful.

During winter, anyone who hasn't been outside for an hour or two will quiz the next person who comes through the door: "How are the roads?" "Roads" is shorthand for a query about snow, ice, freezing rain—and whether you'll risk your life by driving. Even walking is highly treacherous if sidewalks are coated with ice. "Anything melting?" is not a casual question. The answer may decide if an elderly woman will get to the grocery store, or a homeowner will try to roll his garbage can down a steep slope to the curb, or a restive mother with small children can get some outdoor exercise. No wonder we keep asking each other.

Good weather brings not complacency but a vague unease. Midwesterners are realists. Nothing lasts; life is short; the darkness waits. "Sure, it's been a great October," people assure each other, "but we'll pay for it, won't we?" We nervously scan for signs of pending disaster: "Did you read that the squirrels are gathering more nuts than usual? You know what that means!" Maybe not everyone has heard of Calvin, but we know about pleasure, sin, and penance. A long sunny fall, one blue and gold day after another, signals a nasty winter. What no one says, but what I hear as an undertone, is a resigned sigh: What the Lord giveth, the Lord taketh away. Everyone talks about the weather with the kind of reverence, baffled awe, fury, frustration, and resignation that I tend to associate with some of the Old Testament prophets who had to deal with an omnipotent but mysteriously capricious God.

When eighteenth-century poets and philosophers wrote about the changing wheel of fortune that turned men's lives upside down without warning, they weren't usually thinking about weather. But Midwesterners who have never read a word of Pope or Dryden might recognize an affinity to this point of view. Living in the Midwest, we watch the weather as if it might be creeping up treacherously behind one's back—and in fact, it sometimes is. We feel we have to keep an eye on it all the time. What might it do to us? And why, infuriatingly, can't we, in turn, do anything about it?

Since weather is an awesome force we cannot control, many of us want to acknowledge and propitiate it. Even a few of my determinedly sophisticated acquaintances, who would hate anyone to assume they consider spiritual issues, make joking references to "the weather gods" or "the Weather God." "If the weather gods smile on us, we'll have the reception on the lawn," they might say, linking themselves unconsciously to the ancient tribes who worshipped the sun or moon or whatever supernatural forces brought warmth and rain.

The linking of God and weather is not, of course, confined to prehistoric religions. The Bible is full of weather. Since part of a proper bringing-up in Ames, Iowa, during the 1940s and 1950s was fairly regular attendance at Sunday School and church, I read or heard parts of the Bible over and over. The majestic rhythms of the King James version beat steadily into my mind, imprinting its imagery of storms, floods, drought, fiery clouds, and mists. Although I knew little about the actual geographic landscape of Palestine, the Mideast of the King James Bible sounded very much like my own Midwest, given the inclement weather that frequently swept over us both.

"The windows of heaven were opened," pronounced the writer of Genesis, and I could picture the heavy, streaming, pounding rain that drenched our town in a summer storm. When Squaw Creek and Skunk River overflowed and flooded the lowlands in town, I could imagine what Noah might have felt as he looked over the railing of his drifting ark. Part of my own known world had, after all, disappeared under sheets of murky water. The water had risen during the night, coming from some inconceivable source, and it would stay until, also without notice, it would just as mysteriously disappear.

Because the God of the Old Testament was so fearsome, I was not surprised that the weather He wrought was usually baleful. He wielded hail like a weapon. Although I wasn't afraid of hail—it was quite thrilling, in a way, when hard little rocks of ice descended suddenly from the sky—I knew it could cause terrible damage to gardens and to crops. My mother nurtured tender petunias and tomato plants, and hail had ruined them more than once. So when the implacable Lord smote Pharaoh, I knew how bad it was: "The Lord sent thunder and hail, and the fire ran along upon the ground; the Lord rained hail upon the land of Egypt. . . . And the hail smote throughout all the land of Egypt all that was in the field, both man and beast; and the hail smote every herb of the field, and brake every tree of the field." I had been caught in hailstorms; *smote* was just the right word.

God never appeared to anyone in a genial shaft of sunlight. Leading Moses and the Israelites out of Egypt, He hid in a frightening pillar of cloud that by night turned into a pillar of fire. "Yea, He did fly upon the wings of the wind," said Psalm 18. "He made darkness his secret place; his pavilion round about him were dark waters and thick clouds of the skies. . . . The Lord also thundered in the heavens, and the Highest gave his voice; hailstones and coals of fire." As for His enemies, Psalm 11 promised, "Upon the wicked he shall rain snares, fire and brimstone, and a horrible tempest." Anyone who had lived through a full cycle of Midwestern seasons knew about horrible tempests.

This was a God who arranged a whirlwind—not a pleasant summer breeze—to carry Elijah up to heaven. The Creator of weather could, and frequently did, make the earth quake. Surely what he sent to descend upon Job's children was a dreaded Midwestern tornado: "And, behold, there came a great wind from the wilderness, and smote the four corners of the house, and it fell upon the young men, and they are dead: and I only am escaped alone to tell thee."

When I drive through the rural Midwest, I am struck by the resolute starkness of its white-shingled country churches. Tall, simple in outline, with graceful steeples that refuse to bow to storm or lightning, these churches seem to embody an unshakable religious belief. Built on hills or a slight rise, with endless acres of farmland flowing around them, they stand like unwavering beacons on their small tree-dotted islands. At the same time, they appear curiously vulnerable: open, unprotected, deliberately planted in the midst of the weather. Anything that blows across the fields or plains will strike with its full force.

The builders of these sanctuaries knew their Old Testament. Yes, our God suffuses the sky, those churches proclaim, so we cannot escape Him. Yes, a great wind from the wilderness may come. The Lord may send thunder and hail. Fire may run along the ground, and the windows of heaven may open. But we—the church with its steeple says quietly but firmly—no, we shall not be moved: "Therefore will not we fear, though the earth be removed, and though the mountains be carried into the midst of the sea." And maybe those sturdy farmers and villagers who knew their Bibles remembered the stern admonition in Ecclesiastes not to obsess about the weather: "He that observeth the wind shall not sow; and he that regardeth the clouds shall not reap."

Some Sundays our minister in Ames read other passages in which the weather was gentler, more like Iowa spring mornings or summer evenings. I liked the reassurance of the Psalm that promised, "He shall come down like rain upon the mown grass: as showers that water the earth," and I could hear the rejoicing in the Song of Solomon: "For, lo, the winter is past, the rain is over and gone; / The flowers appear on the earth; the time of the singing of birds is come."

When I turned to the New Testament, which seemed so much less threatening than the Old, biblical weather improved. Christ soothed troubled waters—"Then he arose, and rebuked the winds and the sea; and there was a great calm"—and He did not follow his Father's habit of stirring up storms or smiting with wind and hail. In fact, He appeared to accept weather much as we did in the Midwest, as part of a plan that we can't expect to understand. Again and again I heard this passage from the Sermon on the Mount, advising us all to love our enemies: "That ye may be the children of your Father which is in heaven: for he maketh his sun to rise on the evil and on the good, and sendeth rain on the just and on the unjust." When I am driving through the countryside in a heavy rain, watching sheets of water sweep over the fields, I may think of those lines.

What I remember most about the connection between the New Testament and Midwest weather is rain on Good Friday. I knew what had happened on the day of the Crucifixion. "From the sixth hour there was darkness over all the land until the ninth hour," said

Matthew, and afterward "the earth quaked, the rocks were split." From someone, I also gleaned the extraordinary fact that weather on Good Friday revealed a True Sign. Specifically, it always rained, not only in Iowa, but all over the world as well. (I did speculate whether it rained in China.) If rain didn't *quite* fall, the sky would be gloomy and overcast, recalling the dreadful day when "there was darkness all over the land."

I considered this snippet of spiritual arcana seriously for several years, well into my teens, because, in fact, it did happen to rain—or nearly rain—every Good Friday. Although I eventually realized that April weather in Iowa is naturally prone to dampness, I never forgot to look up at the sky on Good Friday. If the sun was shining brightly, I felt, for one brief moment, betrayed. For years I thought this was only a superstition. But recently, when I somewhat sheepishly mentioned it to a friend who is steeped in liberal theology, she replied, quite matter-of-factly, that statistics actually concur. Good Fridays are, she said, rainier than usual. (I am still curious whether they tend to be rainier in China.)

Given my childhood background in biblical verse, enriched by later years of studying literature, it is not surprising I can hear the voice of God in the whirlwind. Not the Old Testament God, exactly. Not a God I can define very clearly. I wish had the faith of those builders of straight unshakable steeples, but I don't. When I left Ames for college, I was lightly cloaked in a kind of vague Presbyterianism, though I had wrongly assumed it was part of my very skin. All it took was the brisk breeze of a course in ancient history, taught by a brilliant and offhand professor who disliked received truths, to blow the cloak almost off my shoulders. Almost, but not entirely.

Although I am seldom called on to describe my beliefs—personal spirituality, as opposed to religion, is a topic few people ask about, at least on the phone, at dinner tables, or over coffee—I never know quite how to do it. I am not comfortable adopting the label "agnostic." It is too cold a word, too excluding, for the kind of faith I wish I could find, something indefinable that glimmers before me, occasionally comforts me, and all too frequently tends to disappear entirely.

Like many people, I can find myself overwhelmed with the demands of daily life. I wake each day to a deserted beach, long and shining, that invites me to walk its length, leaving slow meditative footprints in the damp sand. But before I take a step, the tide sweeps in, bringing with it a load of flotsam and jetsam—bright shining glass, bits of paper, messages in bottles. The tide retreats, and all day I struggle to clean up my stretch of sand. The next morning, before I can set foot on it, the tide comes in again.

On some days, Midwest weather rescues me. No, I am not always thankful for its interruptions—the ice storm that makes me cancel an appointment, the soaring heat that slows me to a soggy crawl, the lightning flash that sends me hurrying indoors. But it does force me to stop and reconsider. Much as I like to think I am in control of my life, I am not. Give it up, take a breather, let it go. I would do well, the inescapable interruption tells me, to remember that there are things I can't fix, puzzles I can't solve, beaches I cannot clean.

Our turbulent, changeable, often disheartening and sometimes magnificent weather does more than stop me in my tracks. It also makes me marvel. The fall wind boisterously thumping against my window, the first thin skin of white ice that forms over our lake one winter night, the mild sun that unfurls my dark-purple violas one spring morning: all of it is wondrously inexplicable. Who could have dreamed up the intricate individual shapes of the snowflakes that effortlessly fall, millions upon millions, and then silently rise in mountainous heaps outside my door? Who thought of making one kind of rain so gentle, so lightly musical, that it can lull a troubled spirit into sleep? How can anyone look at roiling black clouds as they sail across a stormy August sky, torn by sharp-toothed lightning, shaken by deafening thunder, and serenely consider the nature of an impersonal universe?

I do not read the Bible as much as I did when I was young. I certainly don't read it in the same way. Most fundamentalists would say I don't really read it at all. But no textbook on meteorology, no scientific explanation, no physicist's theory about possible beginnings or probable ends has yet replaced for me the King James Bible's haunting rhythms. They describe the very skies under which I live. I am puzzled and alarmed by the prophecies of John the Evangelist, the strange ecstatic mystic of the Book of Revelation. But when John looks to the sky, I can understand at least this part of his vision: "And the temple of God was opened in heaven, and there was seen in his temple the ark of his testament: and there were lightnings, and voices, and thunderings, and an earthquake, and great hail. And there appeared a great wonder in heaven." He might be speaking about Midwest weather.

SUSAN ALLEN TOTH is the author of *Blooming: A Small-Town Girlhood, Ivy Days,* and a trilogy on travel in the United Kingdom: *My Love Affair with England, England As You Like It,* and *England for All Seasons.* She has written personal essays and travel pieces for many newspapers and magazines, including the *New York Times, Washington Post,* and *Los Angeles Times.* She was born and raised in Ames, Iowa, and currently lives in Minneapolis.